The Only Constant

Also by Najwa Zebian

Welcome Home: A Guide to Building a Home for Your Soul

The Only
Constant

A Guide to Embracing Change and Leading an Authentic Life

Najwa Zebian

Published by arrangement with Harmony Books, an imprint of Random House, a
division of Penguin Random House LLC. First published in the United States in 2024

First published in Great Britain in 2024 by Yellow Kite
An imprint of Hodder & Stoughton Limited
An Hachette UK company

4

Book design by Andrea Lau
Interior art by Shutterstock.com/marukopum

A CIP catalogue record for this title is available from the British Library

Hardback ISBN 978 1 399 72060 1
Trade Paperback ISBN 978 1 399 72062 5
ebook ISBN 978 1 399 72061 8

Printed and bound in India by Manipal Technologies Limited

MIX
Paper from
responsible sources
FSC™ C104740

Hodder & Stoughton Limited
Carmelite House
50 Victoria Embankment
London EC4Y 0DZ

www.yellowkitebooks.co.uk

To my grandma, Wajiha,
the light of your heart still guides me.

To my therapist, Brenda,
you helped me unleash my inner wisdom and save my life.

Accept change before it makes you reject your reality.
Choose change before it chooses you.
Embrace change so it can lead you to your authentic life.

Contents

The Only Constant

CHAPTER 1

Why Change Is Hard

Hint: Because we want it to be easy

I will never forget the moment everything changed for me. I've always known that change is hard, whether it's a change I choose or one life chooses for me. I've also always known that change is one of life's only constants. Not just that, change is one of life's most beautiful truths. Change is what puts *life* in our lives. Change is the gateway to authentic transformation.

I don't know about you, but the part I couldn't quite put my finger on for the longest time was this: How on Earth do I actually *embrace* change instead of just knowing and believing that change is an integral part of life? How do I make change beautiful and necessary instead of staying stuck at the intersection of knowing and doing? How do I stop trying to skip the part that is messy, uncertain, and unstable? How do I just *do* change?

How do I go from knowing that I need to live my life authentically to actually living that way? Especially when it means that my life will be flipped upside down in this pursuit? How do I go from knowing that the self-loving thing to do is to leave all toxic relationships behind and believe that I can form healthy connections, to actually doing that? How do I go from knowing that I want a career *I* love, not what my family or friends think is best for me, to actually pursuing it? How do I go from knowing that boundaries are essential for my self-preservation, to not allowing guilt to make me go back on them? How do I go from knowing that grief is healing to actually sitting with it?

There is one thing I know for sure. As Greek philosopher Heraclitus once said, "Change is the only constant in life." You can resist the flow of life, but all that does is keep you living in resistance, going against the current of being alive. Embracing the only constant in life eases your transformation into the person you are meant to be—the most authentic version of yourself.

Life gave me opportunities to try embracing change. And without fail, it will give *you* opportunities to embrace change. I will tell you my stories in this book, and I hope that they help you feel less alone as you confront your own changes—the changes you choose, the ones you don't, and the ones you need to make. But first I want to tell you about a moment that brought it all together for me and taught me five truths about change.

1. Change Is Hard Because We Focus So Much on How Hard Change Is Instead of Seeing It as a Path to the Life We Want

Right before I started writing this book, my grandma passed away peacefully in her sleep. She and my grandpa had been together for seventy-five years.

The day after she died, my mom and I and a few family friends were sitting with my grandpa in his front yard, surrounded by all the beautiful flowers my grandma grew over the years. We sat under the same grapevine where I had spent many childhood hours waiting for its bunches to turn from tiny sour green grapes to big juicy drops from heaven. It was always my grandma who made sure my grandpa picked me the exact one I wanted.

We were all engulfed in the big void of her absence. When you lose someone you love, their absence somehow intensifies how their presence would feel.

It was quiet. We could hear the leaves and the wind make the most peaceful symphony that somehow put us all in a trance of feeling as if my grandma were still there. Then moments would come when we would snap back into reality and tears would just start quietly streaming down our faces. My grandpa's tears carved two streets on his cheeks for his grief to express itself. He had been quietly crying, but this time he said out loud, "How am I going to live without you, my best friend?" A family friend, who I am sure had the best intentions, said, "It's not good to cry. It's like you're saying that you don't accept God's will."

As I was ready to leap in with my speech on grief that went something like, *He is grieving. Let him love her and think of her the way he wants,* my grandpa looked at her. He pointed to a light pole in front of the yard and said, "You see that light pole over there? There were two birds that would come and rest at the top of it every day. One day, one of them flew a bit too low and a stray cat ate it."

He pointed with his finger to the place where it happened.

Then he said, "The other bird still comes here and rests at the top of that pole, facing the exact direction where its partner was killed."

He took a deep pause and said, "If a bird can get sad over another bird, why do you say I can't get sad over the woman I loved for seventy-five years? My best friend."

Goosebumps. Right?

Everyone went quiet. We went back to the sound of the leaves being the only sound any of us could hear.

Regardless of how my grandpa felt, he understood one thing very well: grieving someone is loving them the way you'd love them if they were still here. Even though that love has nowhere to go, you allow yourself to feel it. You allow yourself to miss them and spend time replaying your memories with them. You honor the love you have for them by giving it space within you when it visits.

My grandpa, now in his nineties, wanted to make sure he greeted every person who came to pay their respects. My uncle approached him at one point and told him to go rest and that my uncle and aunts would make sure to welcome everyone. He vehemently refused. He said, "She waited for me every day of her life. I can't wait a couple more hours until everyone who came for her leaves?"

That's love. He was loving her in her absence. He was loving her without any expectation of reciprocation or reward for that love. He was loving her the way he knew she would feel loved. Doing what you know would make your beloved feel loved is love.

As sad as I was, I couldn't help but be in awe of that love. Isn't that what we all want? Someone to love us that way, with that dedication and commitment?

That's the kind of love I always knew I wanted, but it seemed to be reserved for novels and movies. I had never before seen it around me.

In that moment, I started imagining a life where I would have that kind of love.

And that's when everything fell into perspective. I started seeing my life as one big, connected timeline of events with a beginning and end. And to get to the life I wanted, I had to start making changes to the things in between, to align them with my desired reality.

To have a life that contains that kind of love, I had to be willing to make changes that would make that possible. In that moment, I shifted my focus from change in and of itself to the life that change would lead to and open space for.

Boom.

This, of course, eased my feelings around change because it skipped over the part where I actually undergo the change. Because that's the hard part. Isn't it?

Maybe change is hard because we focus so much on achieving the change itself instead of focusing on what that change will achieve for us. It's like we are challenging ourselves to prove that we can do it. When you fight with yourself for your worth, it's an ugly battle. When your focus is, "Can I actually do this?" instead of "I am working toward this," you are making your ability to reach the goal mean something about you. You are likely to judge yourself based on your accomplishment of the goal or how far you've progressed and how far you still have to go. When you stop seeing change as the goal and start seeing change as the path to the life you want, that's when authentic transformation happens.

This leads us to another reason change is hard.

2. Change Is Hard Because We Want It to Be Easy

Sit with these words for a little while. We want the change to happen without having to change anything.

Now think of this with me: If you want a plant in your garden to grow livelier and healthier, you change its environment, right? You might change the soil or add fertilizer to it. You might change the way or frequency with which you water it. You might remove a plant nearby that may be hindering its growth. You might even give it a trim to give room for new growth. Moral of the story is, you don't just keep it as it is and expect it to grow differently. So why do you expect your life to change without changing anything?

I know you know this. And I know you're not a plant. Life is not as simple as adding an ingredient or taking out one. But in between knowing and doing, there is a big distance. That distance can be bridged by believing in yourself and trusting yourself. Your voyage will take you over the waters of your old patterning, your beliefs about yourself, every what-if, every fear, and so on. For most of us, we have to build that bridge of self-belief and self-trust as we are crossing it.

Knowing empowers you. Doing transforms you. The doing, both fueled by and adding to your knowledge, happens in the stretch between where you are now and where you want to be.

The ease of change comes with the acknowledgment and acceptance that to make change happen, you have to be willing to make changes to your current reality. The ease of change comes with the acknowledgment and acceptance that some changes will be hard. And that two things can be simultaneously true: A change can be hard. And it can be done.

Let me give you an example. In *Welcome Home*, I wrote, "The biggest mistake that we make is that we build our homes in other people. We build those homes, and we decorate them with the love and care and respect that we want to come home to at the end of the day. We invest in homes in other people, and we evaluate our self-worth based on how much those homes welcome us. When those people walk away, those homes walk away with them and, all of a sudden, we feel empty because everything that we had within us, we put in those homes. We trusted someone else with pieces of us. That emptiness that we feel doesn't mean that we have nothing to give, or that we have nothing within us. It's just that we built our home in the wrong place."

Maybe you recognize yourself in those words, but you struggle to actually take the steps to build that home within and live authentically as yourself.

I get it. It is terrifying to make the change once you know you need to make it. Because not only will *you* change, but the *you that others see* will also change. And that is scary.

So many of us, for years, want to change something in our lives but feel stuck. And feeling stuck leads us to stagnation. The more time we spend in that "stuck" space, the worse the feeling of being stuck becomes. Because now it's coupled with feeling shame and helplessness. Do we choose change and risk the identity we have now? Or do we stay the same and keep an identity we don't even want anymore?

3. Change Is Hard Because It Causes a Break in the Reality We're Living In

A few months ago, a woman reached out to me. Let's call her Veronica. She was telling me that she finally decided to file for divorce from her husband of more than ten years. Within that story, she told me something that also shifted my perspective on change. It may do the same for you.

She told me she had no idea who she was. She didn't know what music she enjoyed or what food she liked. She said, "I molded myself into exactly who I needed to be to be of service to my husband and kids. I didn't matter. Only they did." She then told me that once it became clear to her husband that she was serious about the divorce, he told her she was definitely having a breakdown.

To me, she said, "I wasn't having a break*down*. I was having a break*through*."

What a beautiful way to see change.

You are not breaking down. You are breaking through. Maybe to break through, you have to have a breakdown—break down the life you currently have in order to build the one you want. Does that mean it's a negative thing? It might be exactly what you need.

So think about this question: Will the change you're contemplating be a breakdown or a breakthrough? The only constant about this change is that it will break the reality in which you are living. But you must understand that this is an essential step in constructing your new reality. Think about it like you are demolishing the space in which you currently reside and rebuilding it on your own terms to look and feel exactly the way you want. The rebuilding requires the demolishing—the breaking.

Veronica told me how difficult the years of her marriage had been. She said she spent all that time trying to derive her worthiness through his validation. She was running a never-ending race that had no finish line. Because as long as she searched for her worth from others, she could never find it.

Even when change is the logical solution that will get you

the inner peace you desire, your body will resist it. That's because your body quite literally feels safer in the presence of the source of pain than when it's disconnected from the source of pain.

I will give you a minute to read that again.

4. Change Is Hard Because We Judge Ourselves for the Choices Our Bodies Make

Maybe you're having a hard time changing because your body is keeping you stuck. It is perceiving change as a threat. You beat yourself up in your mind because you think, *I know better. So why am I accepting this?* Or, *I know this is not like me, but why do I continue to do it?*

I happen to have the answer. No, not strictly from doing research, not from a textbook or anything like that, but from my personal experience of feeling stuck in many relationships that I knew no longer served me. From being stuck in many relationships I knew were toxic for me. (When I talk about relationships, I often get asked, "Does this include relationships with family and friends?" Absolutely. Anytime I mention the word "relationship," I want you to know I'm referring to all kinds of relationships, including workplace and school relationships.)

Those relationships were toxic because being my authentic self with those people meant that I would be in danger of losing those relationships. My welcome in those relationships was conditional on me being a certain way. It was conditional on me keeping secrets about my life. This is not the same as privacy. It is secrecy. When you decide to be private about a certain part of your life only because revealing it would cause great backlash and turmoil, that's not privacy by choice. That's secrecy to protect yourself, and that's what I was doing. I was convinced it was privacy, but if I were to have a heart-to-heart with myself, I knew very well it was fear-driven secrecy.

Sometimes we try so hard to change ourselves and the way we react to those around us that we forget that it should not be this hard to belong. It doesn't matter how much we change ourselves, when we are surrounded by the same people who make us feel that being ourselves is wrong or too much, that change just feels more imprisoning. Because now we know what we are worth. Now we know what we deserve. We know we deserve better. We know we are being treated with conditional love and respect. We know we are being belittled at times and beaten down at times.

Knowing and being aware makes the choice to stay so much harder in relationships that are conditional on our being a certain way. Because now we are *aware* that we are betraying ourselves when we expose ourselves to the toxicity.

You know what I'm talking about, right?

Take the example of being in a relationship, romantic or not, where someone feels comfortable disrespecting you, and the thought that pops into your mind is *You know better. Why are you accepting this?*

And then you go down a spiral of thoughts that go something like *Why do I keep allowing them to treat me this way? Why haven't I put my foot down and actually stuck to it? Why do I keep coming back and allowing this to happen? Why am I betraying myself? Why am I abandoning myself? Why do I care so much about what others think of me?* And so on.

You go down this spiral of judgment and shame, aimed at no one but yourself. Because now you know who you are and what your worth is, but you're still accepting the treatment that you accepted when you were self-abandoning, unaware of your worth.

So, really, why do we do that? Why do we continue to accept the same treatment we did before we truly saw our worth for what it is?

Buckle up because I'm about to change your life. No, really. Because this changed my life.

As I attempted to heal all the moments in my life when I felt I abandoned myself, I asked my therapist, "Why do I continue to allow this to happen? Why am I not living by what I know? Why does my mind know 100 percent that I need to end many relationships, yet I keep them going? Why does ending them somehow feel even worse than the suffering they are causing me?

"My mind decided a long time ago that I need to end these relationships. But I feel like I can't. I keep knocking on the same doors that never open. I judge myself for continuing to knock when I know that the only way those doors will open is if I leave my authentic self at the door. I'm not willing to do that, yet I still come back and knock and feel sad when the doors don't open. Then I judge myself again, and the cycle repeats itself. Why do I continue to choose to abandon myself?"

My therapist said, "Have you considered that maybe you're not choosing to abandon yourself and that maybe your body is choosing what it believes is the safest choice for it?"

When I tell you that my soul left my body but somehow perfectly aligned with it at the same time, I am not exaggerating. I was at a loss for words. My body was at a loss for feeling. My mind was at a loss for thoughts. I just lost awareness of my surroundings.

What? My body has a choice too? My body can actually decide that it wants to stay? Is this body not just controlled by me?

It felt like I knew this, but at the same time, I clearly didn't. I thought that I was betraying myself by keeping those relationships. Instead, I needed to see that my body was making a choice I needed to listen to and honor. All this time, I was listening to my mind, to my logic. I was giving my mind all this attention and energy and listening to it so carefully. But was I doing that for my body? No, I wasn't.

Have you ever gone through an experience like this? Where you knew on a logical level that the best thing for you is to leave (leave a job, relationship, friendship, school program, or something else) but somehow the moment you think of actually leaving, your body gets heavy with tension and immobility? Every person experiences it differently. I feel this overwhelming gravitational pull that makes my body feel heavy. It becomes hard to move. I often find myself heading to my bed or the couch. My hands go into fists. My arms feel tingly. My chest feels tight to the point where I eventually start having a hard time filling my lungs with air. I go into the fetal position, my body folding in upon itself as if it wants to protect itself from something. As a result of feeling this overwhelming response from my body, I avoid feeling this way again by avoiding the decision I know I have to make—to leave. At the same time, I judge myself for not being able to do the right thing.

So this is what I learned from my therapist in that session: You need to honor the choices that your body makes. Don't look at what feels safe for your body with judgment and shame. It's not that you aren't willing to do what your mind knows is best for you, it's that your body still hasn't internalized that what it's living through is actually not safe. It's familiar, but it's not safe. It's not easy for your body to differentiate between familiarity and safety, but the first step toward giving your body that choice is to listen to it.

When you're unconscious of your body's power, the familiar will be the safe choice for your body. But once you start going inward and checking in with your body without judgment, you will realize that your body is actually screaming, *This doesn't feel good*. Once you can start allowing your body to be seen and heard by you, then you can break your body's old definition of "safe." You can break the bond between what is familiar and what is safe. It is only then that your body can start learning a new definition of "safe," one that actually feels peaceful and unconditionally welcoming and loving of you.

Did that blow your mind the way it did mine?

What would you do if someone said to you, "You're stupid"? I'm sure you think you'd immediately stand up for yourself or walk away or just not allow that person to ever have a chance to say that to you again. But that's not what happens in real life, is it? We are great at logically responding to hypothetical situations, but when those situations are real, our response is completely different from what we'd imagine it to be. We start to think, *How could they speak to me this way? What makes them think I'm stupid/selfish/ugly/_____* [whatever words they used to describe you]? *How could they treat me this way?* That line of questioning is your mind trying to make sense of two things:

1. Trying to make sense of the other person.
2. Trying to make sense of why you accepted what they did.

If you really think that there is ever an explanation for someone mistreating you, then you subconsciously believe there is a reason for you to be mistreated. Let's make something very clear! There is never, ever an excuse for someone mistreating you. Period. It doesn't matter what they've been through, how someone else treated them in the past, or what they are currently going through. None of that excuses them projecting onto you that which is not your burden to carry.

When your mind tries to make sense of why you're accepting what you know is not okay, and when you keep that dialogue with yourself at the level of your mind, the only logical explanation you might come up with is, *I am simply not strong enough to stand up for myself.*

The two things you just attempted to do stayed at the level of your mind. Nowhere did you try to bring your body in on the conversation. That's what I did.

I would simply think that if I wasn't able to act upon what I knew, I was consciously betraying myself. Because I know better, how could I not *do* better? Now I know it's because I didn't give my body the chance to know in the same way I gave my mind that chance. Instead of honoring that my body had a choice in all the moments I felt stuck, I judged myself for not doing what my mind knew was the right thing to do.

I told my therapist, "The way I deal with being mistreated is that I tell myself that the behavior of others has nothing to do with me and I need to not take it personally. Then I look for ways to prove that I haven't allowed their words or their treatment to stop me from being myself."

She said, "Could it be that the reason you convince yourself not to take it personally is that your body wants to avoid the pain you would feel if you actually gave yourself the right to feel the pain of that mistreatment?"

Yes?

Yes.

Yes!

You can tell yourself that someone's behavior toward you has nothing to do with you and that it is a direct reflection of who they are, how they feel about themselves, and what they choose. All of that is true. But if someone aims an arrow of mistreatment and harm at you, does the reason it was aimed at you take away from the reality that it will hurt you? No. The reason doesn't take away the harm. Maybe you're so afraid to feel the pain because you ultimately know it will push you to end that relationship, and that's just something you can't even begin to imagine.

When you know there is a change you need to make in your life, whether it's a big or small one, just remember that your body has a choice to make just as your mind does. Your body will not make the choice that your mind has decided is healthy if you don't give it a seat at the table. The most beautiful moment will be when your mind and body are in alignment, when your mind stops judging you and shaming you for not making the changes you know you need to make, and when your mind actually sits with your body and gives it the same compassion and empathy it would give to anyone out there. But to get there, you have to actually *feel* the feelings that flow through your body.

I'm going to give you an example. Later that day, after I spoke to my therapist, I decided to start rewiring the mental pathway that I took every time I did something that I judged myself for (because I was "betraying myself"). That pathway typically went something like:

Being spoken to/treated in a way that disrespects me and my boundaries. → Thinking, "How can I accept this?! How can I allow this to happen again?" → Feeling stuck because I feel like I just can't put an end to this relationship.

I worked on changing it to:

Being spoken to/treated in a way that disrespects me and my boundaries. → Thinking, "How can I accept this?! How can I allow this to happen again?" → Feeling stuck because I feel like I just can't put an end to this relationship. → Turning inward to my body and asking myself, "How does this feel in my body?" → Soothing my body by allowing that sensation to be validated so it can be released. → Setting a boundary for my body by removing it from the environment in which that treatment happened. ("I will leave the room, the house, the space where I was disrespected to give my body time to recover from the pain it just experienced.")

Do you see how the focus in the second scenario was 100 percent about me approaching myself with no judgment or shame? How, instead of feeling "stuck," I gave my body an opportunity to be validated? I gave my body an opportunity to question how good its old definition of "safe" feels?

I gave myself a hug that day. I recalled being told by someone I love that I am selfish for wanting to be included in their expression of love and affection to those whom they love. Instead of judging myself for continuing to give that person access to my life, I immediately went to my body. I closed my eyes and started feeling where the pain was. It was in my chest and my arms. They felt like fire. All I could think was, *This feels awful!* It was so shocking to me because I always knew I became tense when I heard words like that, but I did not know it was this intense. As I felt that fire in my arms and chest, I just sat with those sensations. Every time my mind would try to jump in, I would just say, "Stop." I wrapped my arms around myself and started moving my hands up and down where the pain was in my arms. I started feeling that hug in my chest. The feeling went from being awful to being at peace. At no time did I spend a moment judging myself. Instead, I sat with my body and listened to it and gave it a chance to be seen and heard. The beautiful thing was, I was practicing self-love in the purest form; giving myself the love (the being seen, the being heard, the being tended to) I so badly wanted from others.

From that moment on, everything changed for me in terms of the way I spoke to myself when my actions did not align with my knowledge. I decided that my body is in the process of changing what safety looks like for it. If my body spent thirty years believing that safety is working hard to prove my worth, it'll take time before my body learns that I am worthy just as I am. If my body spent thirty years believing that safety is accepting being excluded because if I spoke up, I'd be shunned and excluded even more, it'll take time before my body learns that being punished for standing up for myself is a sign that I'm with the wrong people and in the wrong place for myself.

If your body has spent X number of years believing that safety is financial security, which is more important than doing something you love, it will take time for your body to learn that leaving a job you're not happy with is okay. If your body has spent years believing that you must be done with school by a certain age, get married by a certain age, or own a home by a certain age, it will take time for it to learn that you get to choose what you want for yourself and *when*. What happens when you follow these expectations is that you will prioritize reaching them over reaching them on your terms, at the right time for you, and with the right people for you.

It's okay to slow down. Learn to tune in and listen to your body instead of constantly judging it for not making the change you've logically decided is right for you. One thing we are not going to do is try to shame ourselves into change. Because you know what that does? It only makes the shame grow and pushes the change farther away. Even if we were to change as a result of shame, that change would not be authentic, and going back to our situation before the change is highly likely. What's driven by shame is sustained by shame. And what's driven by compassion is sustained by compassion. Show yourself compassion. Be kind to yourself as you go through change.

This doesn't just apply to relationships with family, friends, romantic partners, coworkers, or schoolmates. This also applies to the physical environments of which you are part, to the stages of your life or the career you are in and to *any* change that feels like you'd rather the world end than having to make that change.

Let's say you have a relationship with a family member that is draining you. Say this family member is highly controlling. To realize this, maybe you had to go through a period of being aware of how toxic the dynamic has been. Your mind, and perhaps friends or a therapist, might tell you that you need to put an end to this toxic dynamic. You might agree, but you have no idea how to go about this. For a time, you might feel stuck. And after a while, you might feel like a broken record, repeating to your friends and confidants how much you want to put an end to this relationship, but how difficult it is, how frustrating it is. This might lead you to judge yourself for not being able to do what is best for you.

This is where I will remind you to slow down. It takes time to remove from your life a person who was there for so long. That time is human and natural. Change is not as simple as realizing you need to change. It is not as simple as knowing what is best for you. Change takes time, because as it's happening, it is forcing you to change at a cellular level. The way your body operated for so many years is changing. What feels right and wrong, or safe and dangerous in your body is changing. Be patient with yourself and with your change. Take a moment right now to look at yourself, in whatever turmoil you're in, and say to yourself, *I see how hard you're trying. I see how hard this is on you. You are making progress. I'm proud of you. You are getting stronger every day, and you will get to the point where you can trust yourself in the decision you need to make.* Take a moment to feel the feelings in your body as a result of saying these words to yourself.

How do you apply this knowledge to any change in life that is within your control? How do you apply this to changing your life plans or changing the program you're enrolled in at school, changing your relationship with your family and friends, changing the place where you live, and so on?

If you also feel "stuck," remember that your body is following a pattern it's developed over the years, and that you absolutely must recognize that patterning and align what your mind knows with how your body feels.

Simply ask yourself, *How does thinking about making this change feel in my body?*

This question will lead you to understand why change scares you so much.

How many times have you contemplated changing your job or your school program but felt "stuck" in the position you're currently in because you were afraid that you're making a big mistake by letting go of something you worked so hard for, or something that others wish they had, or something that your parents or guardians really wanted you to do? Maybe you feel that fear is what's keeping you in your place.

Let me tell you the story of how I changed my career path at the age of twenty-six. I spent four years getting a bachelor's in science (I hated my life during that time) and a whole year getting my bachelor's in education so I could teach. I spent an additional year completing my master's in education, because why not? Then I applied for a doctorate in education twice before I got accepted. Imagine getting all of that accomplished, paying all of that money for school, which amounts to at least $150,000, and then saying, "Well, I changed my mind. I want to write."

How could it be that I spent seven years (at that point) in university only to figure out that it's not actually what I wanted to do? I mean, I loved teaching. I still do. But writing truly is my passion. Putting words to feelings and thoughts. It's what I can do all day, every day, without feeling tired, even though it drains me. Plus, how do I go from a job that is secure, with great medical benefits, with summers and all holidays off, to a job that is not the slightest bit as secure or lucrative?

It just felt extremely unnatural. At that time, not having the level of awareness I do now, I took that risk because the pain of not writing was much bigger than the pain of writing. I allowed myself to give more time to my writing and took on fewer teaching assignments, which enabled me to teach in a much bigger classroom . . . the classroom of the world.

The journey made me realize that when you spend so much

of your life working toward a certain goal and at some point you want to change the path you're on, the fears that keep you in your place are inevitable. You might wonder if throwing away all that you've already worked for is the smart thing to do, or you simply might see all that you've already worked for as a waste of time. You might wonder if this means that you're not grateful enough for what you have: *What will others think of you? Will they see you as a failure? What if you actually do fail on this new path you'd like to take? And worse, what if you fail and then have to start over on the old path you were on?* All of these thoughts and questions will cross your mind, and the reason you feel stuck is that you quite literally don't know the answer to any of them.

It's the not knowing, the uncertainty, that keeps you in your place. Just like your body doesn't differentiate between "safe" and "familiar" until you start listening to it, it also doesn't differentiate between "unsafe" and "uncertain" until you start listening and understanding why it ties those two words together. Maybe you were raised in a way where mistakes were punished. Maybe you were raised in a way where being your own person was highly criticized because you had to be a certain way. Maybe you were raised in a way that taught you to achieve certain milestones by a certain age. What's the *story*? What's *your* story? Ask yourself that. Because the truth is, and you know this, nothing in your life will change if you don't change something about what you're doing. So what's truly stopping you?

This leads us to the next reason why change is hard.

5. Change Is Hard Because We Want Others to Validate Our Choices

The choices we make for ourselves are often shaped by the opinions of those whose approval we want. Maybe your parents expect you to live your life a certain way. Maybe your partner places conditions on the love they give you based on what they want for you or from you. The interesting thing is that your body finds safety in whatever looks like the love and acceptance that you were taught when you were young. So this turns into what feels safe in your body while your body is unaware of the distinction between what's familiar and what's safe.

We repeat the patterns we developed with our parents (or those who cared for us at a young age) with others in our adult years because we are trying to change the outcome of what we believe about ourselves through changing those patterns. So now we get stuck trying to get the approval of friends or a boss or a partner hoping that the reward will be the validation and approval we were conditioned to seek. Maybe you tried so hard to get the love of your father by succeeding in school because his love was conditional on your achievements. Now, as an adult, you'll do the same with partners. Hence why you seem to attract partners who have the same conditions placed on the love they offer you. What's even sadder is that you try to change your partner into someone who doesn't condition their love on your achievements to prove to yourself the opposite of what your father conditioned you to believe . . . that you deserve love without the achievements. It could also be that you are subconsciously seeking the familiarity of your childhood patterning, as it feels safe in your body, because you always know the outcome and because you feel the same bond you felt with your father.

Sometimes the things that stop us from going after what we want are so much bigger than us, like culture and religion. We might face exclusion at a much larger level, or not just exclusion, but also shame. When your goodness as a human being, or in my case, as a woman, is equated with how well you follow certain rules that are often gender-specific, change that would be otherwise *just* hard, is *exceptionally* hard, hard in a way that you feel like your whole life will fall apart if you make one small change.

For example, moving out of your parents' home at a certain age before you get married is culturally acceptable and, for the most part, expected in North America. But that topic isn't even on the table for many. I want this book to be inclusive of every human's struggles when it comes to change. While the specific reasons we fear change might be different, it really is all the same. We all want to belong. We want to feel like we are part of something. We want to feel like our truest, authentic, unfiltered self is fully and wholly accepted, loved, and seen.

I recently read about Sania Khan, a twenty-nine-year-old South Asian woman who decided to leave her abusive marriage. By her own account, her community shunned her, her family shamed her, and she was left to believe that leaving the marriage was a huge mistake. Months after she went public with sharing those details, her ex-husband drove across state lines to her apartment and murdered her with a gun. So when I speak about the distinct challenges presented by culture, religion, and gender norms, I don't speak lightly.

When change comes at odds with the culture or religion into which you were born, and when you know you will get backlash and exclusion for your choices, there is a huge deterrent to making that change. I went through that. I realized that if someone's religious beliefs or the culture they follow pushes them to shame and exclude you, do you really want to be welcomed and included by that person? Why is it that you carry the burden of keeping that relationship? Why can't it be a two-way street? If staying in someone's life is 100 percent your responsibility through following certain rules or traditions, that's conditional acceptance and conditional love. In no way will it nourish your authentic self. Instead, it will tell your authentic self to sit in the corner for a time-out whenever it tries to shine through.

You have the right to your own relationship with God, if you believe in God. You have the right to your own spirituality. You have the right to your own humanity. Don't let anyone brainwash you into believing that God accepts you or loves you only in a certain way. You don't know that. They don't know that. Only God knows that. Someone's choices to use religion or culture as an excuse to shame or exclude you for a choice you made for yourself is not someone who honors you as your own unique person. And if shame and exclusion is their way of getting you to stay on a certain path or get on a certain path, they are pushing you to change for them, not for you.

When it comes to change that includes these big, scary factors, you must decide what you believe in. Those who respect and love you will show they won't make their acceptance of you dependent on your compliance.

A few years ago when I decided to take off my hijab, I remember telling my therapist at the time, "I keep getting asked the same question in different ways, 'What's special about you now?' as if the only thing that made me special was that I was a visibly Muslim woman who writes. And now that I am no longer visibly Muslim, I have somehow given up the only thing that made me unique."

Looking back at that now, the question was an insult in so many ways. But at the time, all I could feel was the pain of disappointing everyone, the pain of not being seen as special or unique anymore. Because I so heavily based the way I saw myself on the way those whose approval I wanted saw me. Even though I knew that this change brought me closer to my authentic self and to what I truly believed about the world, I still felt as though I had nothing to define me anymore.

You've probably experienced a version of this question in your life too. Maybe the thing that made you special is how you're always there for everyone and never say no. And when you attempt to start setting boundaries and stating your wants and needs, you are made to feel like you lost that special thing that earned you acceptance and approval before. But is it really acceptance and approval if it leaves no space for you to be yourself? If it leaves no space for you to expect to be treated in a way that reflects the worth you know you have? Please think about that.

If those around you only see a specific thing about you as special, they might feel entitled to tell you that you lost whatever it is that makes you special. Losing that, whatever it is, could keep you stuck in your place for a long, long time.

How about we drop the "now" in that question. Let's ask, "What's special about you?" Instead of looking for that one thing that makes us special in the current context, which imprisons us even more, we can be special all the time. Not in an arrogant or stuck-up kind of way, but in a confident, at-home-with-ourselves kind of way. As long as you think that only certain labels make you special, you will feel you're paying a heavy price to make changes and become your authentic self. You may be less likely to make authentic changes because you'd rather be *seen as special* than *feel and know you are special* without needing the outer world to validate that for you.

So the next time someone asks you in any way, "What's so special about you *now*?" . . .

What's so special about you now that you left your marriage?

What's so special about you now that you dropped out of that program?

What's so special about you now that you decided you don't want to have children?

What's so special about you now that you no longer carry that one label that made you stand out?

Let your answer be: *Me*. That's what's always been and what will always be special about you.

I also find it amusing that "What's special about you now?" turns into "So you think you're special now?" when you do something that makes you stand out. Say you came out to the world with a different gender identity or sexual orientation. Say you built a successful business. Say you pursued a career path that is dominated by the opposite sex. The same people who would ask, "What's special about you now?" would ask, "So you think you're special now?" because both questions are intended to shame you into feeling that your change was wrong... that *you* are wrong.

Sometimes we are the ones asking ourselves those questions. For example, think of how lost some parents feel after their children grow up and lead their own lives. They're so wrapped up in their identity as parents that they forget who they are beyond that. Or when someone's worked their whole life and feels like they can't retire because they can't see themselves outside of what they do. When we pride ourselves on being something or doing something, we might feel a big part of us is lost once that thing is gone. Similarly, when we get to a place in life where we really want to be, we might allow those same voices to make us feel guilty for the change that is now in our life. Once you have this awareness, make sure you're not the one asking yourself, "What's special about you now?" and "So you think you're special now?"

It is you who will lead your life. It is you who will make the changes you desire and the changes that you know you need to make. It is you who will live through changes you have no control over. So let it be you who makes decisions for yourself, and let it be you who is your best friend and biggest cheerleader as you make those changes.

Change is the necessary path to the life you want. Hardship, or lack of ease, at least, is natural. When we start changing what we normally do, it's common to experience struggle, especially if you're pushing yourself out of your comfort zone. It will feel like an uphill battle, like a mountain you're carrying when you really should be climbing it. Notice how both carrying and climbing are hard, but the former makes your life harder over time and the latter moves you toward an easier life.

Any break in your reality, which constitutes change, forces you to pause or fully stop. It might feel like your life is slowing down or taking a completely different direction. And that's uncomfortable. Your body might perceive that change as a threat. Because it presents a novelty that your body is not used to. Anything new will be something that your body resists, especially if your body is living in survival mode. Oftentimes, when we struggle with making a change, we judge ourselves for being "weak." The truth is, our bodies have the power to make a choice just as our minds do. So wanting to make a modification that you feel you just can't is not a sign of weakness. If anything, it's a signal that your body is holding on to your current state out of fear. Oftentimes, the fear is an indicator that your body's survival mode limits are being pushed; you feel that you won't be able to survive this change actually taking place. It could be that you connect your survival to the attachment you have to those whose validation you really want.

Start seeking validation from within. That might be hard because you don't really know who you are. So, make a goal to get to know yourself as you would someone that you're meeting for the first time. Get in the habit of tuning in to your body and asking yourself, *What am I feeling right now? Where is this coming from? What do I need right now?* Getting to know who you are will make it easier for you to believe the validation that comes from inside. It allows you to build a bond of trust with yourself.

The bigger the change for which you are aiming, the harder it is to move through it. Don't let that make you believe that it's wrong to go forward with the change. See it as your body's natural reaction. This removes the pressure to be 100 percent certain that this change will lead you to the outcome you want. Moving forward, remove your expectation that change will be easy. Tell yourself, *This is hard, and I can do it!*

CHAPTER 2

What Stops Us from Changing

"You are the only one standing in your way." I've heard these words so many times, and, without fail, they've always made me feel misunderstood. *What do you mean I am the only one standing in my way? There's this person, that pain, that system of power, that way of thinking, that rule, that expectation, and so on.* I couldn't comprehend how someone would blame me for struggling to move forward in my life. For stumbling with letting go of all that was holding me back. It all felt like it was so much bigger than me.

I understand a person's intention when they say something like that is to empower you to lead your life. But the part they often miss is that their statement dismisses the complexity of the tug-of-war happening between who you've been and who you want to be. It dismisses the conflict that happens between the patterns of thinking and behaving that you followed for so long and the ones you want to follow. When we struggle with change, we want to hear words of encouragement and empowerment, not ones containing a hidden message that we're not being strong enough.

I'm sure when someone tells you that you're the only one standing in your way, their intention is to remind you that you have the power to change your life when you decide to be the decider, the chooser, the leader. Here's what this approach misses: Understanding that what stands in the way of you becoming your own leader is not weakness or a lack of willingness. It's a mountain of conditioning from your life to seek approval for your change. Not changing is rarely ever about not *wanting* to change. It's more about not *believing* you have the ability to live through the change. Think of one change that you've been contemplating and close your eyes and feel the sensations that go through your body as you imagine making the modification. You might feel crippling anxiety rushing through you.

You know what it is that stops you from changing. You know the thoughts and emotions that bubble up. These are messengers telling you what your obstacles are. So listen to them. The more you tune in to what your body and mind are telling you, the better you'll be able to understand yourself. You'll be better equipped to separate reality from your perception of reality. And remember, although some obstacles are unique to each person, other obstacles are common to us all. Here, I will talk about a few common obstacles we face on our journey to change.

1. Uncertainty

I had a friend in high school who once shared with me the story of her sister Tanya. She told me that Tanya was one of the most beautiful girls in their community. She was in her early twenties at the time, educated with a university degree, and had a job of her own. A man from her community was interested in marrying Tanya, so he brought his family to seek her hand from her parents. This man wasn't educated, but he came from a wealthy family. He even drove a Ferrari. Tanya fell in love with him very quickly and very deeply. She was so excited for them to marry and start their life together.

My friend was telling me this story because she had woken up to Tanya crying hysterically one morning. And when she asked her what was going on, Tanya said that her fiancé had gone out partying all night and that she was pretty sure he cheated on her. A girl texted her from an unknown number saying, "I have your man." She was heartbroken.

My friend told me that her parents told Tanya to leave him, whether or not he cheated, because this kind of behavior (going out all night without answering his phone) is not what you accept from a man you want to marry.

Over the next few months, my friend would update me on Tanya's situation. Day after day, her sister would wake up to flowers at the door, multiple phone calls, messages, and handwritten letters. He and his family tried very hard to get Tanya back.

Tanya kept saying no, because going back to him would mean that she willingly went back to someone who showed her a big, intensely red flag. Even though she still loved him and struggled with the idea of letting go of a future with him, she couldn't bring herself to accept him, especially with her whole family now against it.

A few months had gone by when my friend came to school and told me that she was leaving early because she had to go with her mom and pick out a dress for her sister's bridal shower. Apparently, Tanya had decided that she was going to give it a shot because this guy tried so hard for months to get her back and promised that he would never betray her again.

Do you think she made the right choice? Do you think they ended up going through with the wedding? And do you think he cheated on her again?

Not knowing the end of this story probably bothers you, right? And that's why uncertainty keeps us stuck.

Uncertainty is simply not knowing, and not knowing is scary. We love security and are more likely to try for something if the outcome is guaranteed. One of the biggest reasons we are so uncomfortable with uncertainty is that we assume the worst will happen. I grew up hearing resilient people described as ones who, no matter where you throw them, land on their feet. I think what we do is look for assurances that we will land on our feet before we take that risk. That we will land in a better place. That we will land, period. And that's why we end up taking familiar roads, not new ones riddled with uncertainty.

Taking the familiar road feels good as we are walking it because we know what it looks like. We know where everything is. Where to turn. Where to stop. Where to slow down. We know how to get back to the start in case things don't work out. We know where to hide when it rains and where to bask in the sun when the sky is clear. That's why knowing feels a lot safer than not knowing. Imagine you accidentally turn onto a whole new road where you have absolutely no idea where things are. You don't know where to stop in case it starts raining heavily or where to get a flat tire changed. You don't know anyone on that road with whom you can go to spend time, and you don't know any places where you can eat or drink. Stop signs don't look the same; neither do lights. There are different and new ways of operating. And worse, imagine you don't know where the road leads. Of course you will feel unsafe, and every cell in your body will want to go back to a road you know—one you recognize.

But you know what the tragedy is? You go back to that familiar road, and it feels great that you are finally back to a place where you have the safety of *knowing*. But every single time—I reiterate: Every. Single. Time—you are hit with the same disappointing end . . . the end to which this road has always led you.

Whether it's operating from your childhood wounds or working a job where you follow and never lead or working so hard to please your parents, your friends, or your partner . . . you will always get to the same end. You can drive a different car. You can dress differently. You can take the backroads for a change. But the road is still the same. The destination is still the same.

And that's one of the most humbling lessons you'll ever learn in your life. You think that changing yourself will make the road's destination align with you. But if that road always leads to a place where you realize your authentic self is not welcome, it doesn't matter what you change. You need to stop deviating so much from who you are to make the road fit.

People who finally leave toxic relationships often hear, "Why did you keep going back?" Well, think about the road. In fact, apply the familiar-versus-unfamiliar-road metaphor to any kind of change in life.

- Why did you stay in a career that you knew you hated for so long?
- Why did you keep that one friend in your life?
- Why did you stay in that college program?

All those questions have the same answer: certainty.

You stayed because you *knew* where those paths would lead based on where they've already led you.

You stayed because you felt safe in the knowing.

This doesn't mean that you *were* safe. You *felt* safe. And the truth is that a road that just *feels* safe because of its familiarity will never *be* safe for the authentic you.

Think of all the places you might discover if you just allow yourself to be unanchored and undefined. You might find places that you didn't even know existed. You might find places you have only heard of before. And you don't know what places you might fall in love with. That's the beauty of embracing uncertainty. So be unanchored. Enjoy the uncertainty. Find new places to which you may choose to anchor yourself for a while.

The solution to the fear of uncertainty is simply choosing it instead of having it forced upon you. For example, say, "I choose a new path for myself, and that means uncertainty is inevitable. I recognize that it can be scary, but I also recognize that it is a necessary ingredient for change."

I have a friend, Alessia, whose story of change truly inspires me. She is very talented at hairstyling. She's the kind of person who will make sure you leave her chair feeling like the most beautiful person in the world. Her problem was that she worked for someone who took advantage of that. Her boss got her to do free work on weekends, all under the guise of giving her free experience. And day after day, she contemplated leaving but worried about the consequences of that: *What if she gives me a bad reference? What if I don't find a job at a better salon? What if I lose all of my clientele?* She was stuck in this what-if loop for well over a year. As an outsider, you might think, "It's just a hair salon. There are a billion hair salons out there."

Feeling trapped is the reality for so many of us. We get so trapped in the stuck feeling that the way out seems to drift farther and farther away from us. And what's worse is that we sometimes gaslight ourselves out of our own worries by minimizing the feeling of being stuck. We say things like, *Maybe it's not as bad as I'm making it seem. At least I have a job at a high-end place like this. I shouldn't leave because I might never find another opportunity like this.* We make the solution so much harder in our minds than it is in reality. Instead of trusting the voice inside that is screaming at us to leave, we trust all the other voices telling us that we don't know what will happen if we do, that tell us that the uncertainty will be even worse.

Here's the truth. The uncertain path holds the possibility of positive outcomes as well as negative outcomes. Even if the outcome is negative, like not getting a better job or not getting into a better relationship or not enjoying a new program, we learn something about ourselves. That way, we become closer to ourselves.

I'm not trying to tell you to go blindly into change and that, no matter what, it will lead to a positive outcome. I'm saying if change is that important to you, if the place you're in is that bad, then change is worth a shot. Are you risking losing what you have now? Absolutely. But if what you have now is causing you turmoil and suffering, or even just unease, what's the harm in attempting to move away from it?

I used to believe that a smart person learns from other peoples' mistakes. I realize now how detrimental that belief was to my growth as a person. Thinking that way made me hyperfocused on not making mistakes. The definition of "mistake" in my eyes was anything that hindered my progress in life—progress toward milestones I didn't even come up with myself.

One of the first books that I read in my teens was *The Alchemist* by Paulo Coelho. I remember being fascinated by the revelation at the end of the novel that the treasure that Santiago sought through the entire book was exactly at the place where he started. Does that mean that his journey—all the experiences he gained and all the people he met—were a waste? Does it mean that all the lessons he learned along the way were useless? And that all the wisdom he gained was pointless?

The takeaway is that the journey you take from where you currently are to where you want to be or to figure out where you want to be is more important than the destination itself. Though the destination may be no different from the place where you originally were, it is yourself who will be different. It is your growth, which could mean a shift in perspective for the value of your current reality or in your value system altogether, that will be different.

Remember my friend Alessia who was worried about leaving her job at the salon? Well, she finally left right at the beginning of the pandemic, so her prospects for getting another job were much worse. But she did it because she was finally fed up with being treated as if she were less than. She was fed up with coming home every day and complaining. She was fed up with knowing that she deserved better but not living by it. So, she chose to be okay with the uncertainty. She left that job without having another job lined up outside of working from home. She decided that it was better to be in the in-between space than to continue to be belittled, disrespected, and taken advantage of. And she decided that she was going to invest the time, energy, and emotional labor into herself. She is a very strong-willed person, but the poisonous work environment had her reacting in ways that didn't feel like herself.

She started looking for jobs over the next few weeks. She was worried about getting a job at a place that wasn't as high-end as the one where she worked, not because she was a shallow person but because she thought that working at a high-end salon meant something about how great of a hairdresser she was. And once she finally accepted a job offer at a new salon that wasn't as high-end as the one before and began working, she realized that at the end of the day, what brings her joy is being able to do what she loves and putting a smile on the faces of her clients.

Uncertainty is uncomfortable but necessary to embrace in order to keep walking ahead with the conviction that we must do the required work to get to a place we want in life. We must get rid of our attachments to the familiar and comfortable.

2. Fear

Fear is what happens when we are convinced that the worst possible outcome of change will happen. We are unsure of the outcome, but we still assume that the worst one is certain. So instead of trying, we stop ourselves to avoid the worst possible scenario. And the worst possible scenario is one that we don't believe we can survive. That's why we commonly hear, "I'd rather die than do this."

Think of the following phrases. How would you end them?

What if I start a new business and . . . ?

What if I get out of this relationship and . . . ?

What if I leave this program and . . . ?

What if I move to a new place and . . . ?

I originally wrote outcomes for these that I consider negative but then remembered that for each of us that negative outcome is different. For example,

What if I start a new business, and it doesn't make $100,000 in the first year?

What if I start a new business, and it doesn't make me more money than what I earn at my current job?

What if I start a new business, and it doesn't do better than that other business?

What if I start a new business, and all the money I put into it goes to waste?

I don't know what your personal worst-case scenario is for any change that you're contemplating, but I will tell you that

47

whatever the fear is, it's valid. It's okay to fear the worst possible outcome. But it's necessary that we aim to not only validate the fear but move forward from it. You can be afraid and still move forward with change. You can also be afraid right until the point when you get the outcome, even if that outcome is not what you expected. You can never guarantee the outcome of anything in life, neither should you be so fixated on it. What you can guarantee is promising yourself that you will do your best to survive after it.

Let me give you an example that I know will hit home for many of you.

In 2016, I gave a speech at the Summit of Greatness in Columbus, Ohio. Right after my speech, there was a meet and greet. People lined up to speak with the speakers from that day. Most of those who lined up to see me didn't just come to say hello but also asked questions.

There's one question I still vividly remember. A woman came up to me and said, "How do I trust again? I was in a long-term relationship, and I got cheated on multiple times. Every time I think of trying to put myself out there to date again, I get so scared of being cheated on that I just don't do it. Even if I get myself to the point where I do date and get into a relationship, I have a hard time staying in it. I pull away and sabotage it. But in my mind, that's better than being hurt all over again. Because I never want to experience that kind of pain again."

This woman was in real pain. I could see it on her face. She was genuinely terrified of being hurt again. But the way she was speaking made it clear that she was certain that the worst possible scenario would happen, that if she were to get into a relationship, she would definitely get cheated on.

So this is what I said to her, and I hope you can take something from these words: "You can never guarantee that someone won't cheat on you. What you can guarantee is that you will choose how to react in a self-respecting, self-loving way if that were to ever happen again. The reason that someone cheating on you hurts so much is not up for negotiation. It hurts. No amount of preparation for it will take the pain away. You hurt because you trusted someone and that trust was broken. You hurt because you were vulnerable with someone and then you were treated as if that vulnerability meant nothing. You hurt because you imagined a certain life with someone and now the reality that you're living in is blurry."

Knowing that you can survive beyond heartache is key. Knowing that your worth is not equal to someone's decision to be unfaithful to you is key. Knowing that you will not accept being with someone who might hurt you in such a way is key.

You can apply this to all other contexts that involve being afraid that history will repeat itself if you try again. The ultimate remedy for fear is self-trust.

But how do I trust myself? By seeing yourself as the leader of your life. And trust that as difficult and dark as times may get, you will be able to take the steps required to get to the other side. Oh, and before you tell me that you can't trust yourself, let me ask you, "How many people have you trusted to get you to your desired destination (physically or metaphorically)?" If you can trust someone else, you can trust yourself. If you can give someone whom you trusted, and who let you down, some grace when they don't uphold that trust, you can do the same for yourself. You'll never be perfect at leading your life, but neither is any other leader out there.

When we allow fear to take the wheel in our lives, we become cautious with everything we do. We anticipate danger at every corner. When fear is in control, its goal is to keep us safe. That safety means anything new or unfamiliar will be perceived as a threat. So even though our current situation might be one we no longer want, our need for safety steers our direction. We fall into patterns that lead to outcomes we already know in our attempts to keep ourselves safe and protected. We resign ourselves to employing patterns that have served us until now. For example, if people-pleasing kept us from facing the consequences of raising our voice, we might fall into people-pleasing again to keep that version of safety—safety that is protective, not welcoming of who we are. And that distinction in the definition of "safety" is the difference between living in survival mode and living in thriving mode. To *survive* means you just want to get by. You don't shine or allow your authentic self to exist. To *thrive* means you want to be fully present as yourself. You don't settle for just what your environment teaches you to *be*, you strive to know who you *are*. When you decide to lead the way and change the definition of what is new and unfamiliar from scary to exciting, then you are more likely to attempt to change your life.

I remember a conversation I had with another therapist when I was going through the change of discovering who I really am as a person outside of my religious and cultural conditioning. I told her I couldn't understand why my family showed so much resistance to any kind of change that I contemplated or attempted, such as moving out before I was married and later taking off my hijab. She told me something that I still visualize every time I get that kind of resistance or shame from the people around me. She said, "You are growing exponentially. Think of a plant that just keeps growing and growing and growing because it was moved into a bigger pot. You are just growing and blossoming into the world, and that scares those who want to keep you a certain way to feel better about themselves. Maybe they define their goodness as people or their being enough as people by the controlled image they have of you. The only way for you to not get that resistance is to stay stagnant and small without growing, and to live by the conditions that they've decided are the limits of who you can be to deserve their acceptance and approval."

At the same time, I understood it was fear that kept me in my place for months, contemplating different changes in my life, even though I knew at my core that those changes were necessary. I also understood that it was fear that pushed my family to be resistant to my change. It's not that they wanted to control me; it's that they were afraid of change just as much as I was, if not more. This approach helped me to show compassion for the upbringing they had and for the conditioning they received and also allowed me to show compassion to myself and not shame myself for changing. Or not judge myself for taking as long as I did to make the changes that I knew I needed to make.

Because I lived in Canada, there was a part of me that felt like deciding to move out at the age of twenty-seven was something that didn't have to be so hard, because it's so normalized. I remember sitting in different circles of people where I would hear them say things like, "I just can't wait for my children to move out at eighteen." Or "My son is twenty-two, and he's still living at home." They would talk about it in a way that showed they were ashamed because it somehow showed that their son had no sense of responsibility. Whereas here I was at twenty-seven years of age, working full time, having established myself in the world, and I was feeling ashamed for the complete opposite of that. For even contemplating moving out before I was married. There was always a part of me that felt that this change shouldn't be so hard. With time, I realized that I was falling into the exact mistake that I urged people not to fall into: deciding how hard change should be based on how hard or easy it was for other people. Just because someone took a certain amount of time to get through something, it doesn't mean that you should take that amount of time too. Similarly, just because a certain change is easy for someone, it doesn't mean that it should be easy for you. You must be willing to see your story as a unique one and to see that story through your eyes and your experience and the environment that shaped it.

So, if there is a change you are contemplating and you are afraid, remember that what you are most likely afraid of is your own growth and evolution and whatever obstacles you will face as you come into yourself. But at the end of the day, you must be more excited about the growth, the blossoming, and the evolution than you are afraid of the reactions you will get.

Remember, trusting yourself means the change is about *you.*

Another way to think of self-trust is conviction—being a person who has firm beliefs and values for yourself and who puts those personal beliefs and values above the opinions of those around you. Now that I've said that, I feel like I'm describing a narcissist or someone who is resistant to influence. That's not what I mean in this case. What I mean is, don't let anyone bully you into believing that you don't have the ability to have your own ways of thinking, being, and living. Don't let anyone coerce you into following their beliefs about what is best for you. You don't want to live a life riddled with guilt every time you contemplate thinking for yourself. You have the right to your own thoughts about yourself and the world around you. You have the right to take your time figuring out what you believe and what you don't believe.

When you find yourself in fear of change, and worry that

taking the leap will do more harm than good, try asking yourself this question:

What if the safety net appears after I jump?

Maybe you're afraid of leaving a relationship that has turned toxic to your well-being. Maybe you're afraid that you won't be able to live without that person. Maybe you're afraid that you will feel ten times worse than the way you already feel with them. And maybe you're just not sure what will happen afterward.

But what if the answer appears *after* you take the risk of asking the question and going to seek the answer? A better outcome may appear once you leave the place where you are now. The dark road ahead could light up bit by bit with every forward step you take.

Isn't that better than the *What if I jump and fall flat on my face?*

Both options are possible, but why think of the worst-case scenario? Why not assure yourself that should you fall, you can trust yourself to get back up?

Not only did this question critically alter how I view change, it also fundamentally recast the way in which fear and uncertainty kept me stuck in my place.

3. Lack of Self-Acceptance and Self-Awareness

We are all shaped by environments that teach us the "right" way to be and think. Our environments teach us the limits of what we are capable of. The journey of growing into our true authentic self requires not only a process of asking what it is that we want but first a process of unlearning. There has to be a process of self-discovery and awareness of all the factors that have shaped us into who we currently are. Without that awareness, we might fall into believing that what we want for ourselves is what we were taught we *should* want.

The process of unlearning necessitates an acknowledgment that we didn't just come to be who we are, but that we are a product of everything we have learned consciously and subconsciously since the moment we came to this life. I remember being told in school that asking questions about why certain rules were put in place by God meant showing disbelief in God. And that I should just trust that if God said we should do something, then that must be the right thing to do. But then I would wonder, *But how do we know that that's what God said, and why would God not want us to know the reasons for certain things?* If I didn't continue to ask questions and give myself permission to have my own beliefs, you wouldn't be holding this book in your hands.

Allow yourself to be a curious person. Allow yourself to ask questions. Allow yourself to wonder why it is that you live the way you live and why it is that you believe certain things are right and wrong. Even if that contemplation leads you to be convinced that that way of living is proper, now, at least, you are a person of conviction as opposed to being a follower. It's a win-win situation for you.

If you read my book, *Welcome Home*, you'll remember that the foundation of a home within is made of self-acceptance and self-awareness. And the basic reason I decided on that was, if you don't know who you are, and if you are not in full acceptance of who you are, then the home that you are building within is for someone you don't know and for someone you believe is inherently flawed. When I use the term "self-acceptance," I don't mean it in the "I am who I am. I have absolutely no work to do on myself. There is nothing that I need to do in my life" kind of way. I mean it in the sense that you accept yourself as you are, as you are changing, as you are breaking, as you are healing, as you are evolving into the person you know you want to be. It's not about being full of yourself. It's more about accepting every part of yourself—the good, the bad, the in-between, the healed, the healing, the broken, the breaking, the growing, the evolving, and the imperfect parts.

Without awareness, you will be ruled by your subconscious beliefs. What that means is that you will be controlled by all that's led you to be who you are today. Awareness allows you to understand yourself and the reason you react in certain ways. In other words, awareness gives you the key to being the leader of your life. You get to choose based on your awareness of what you want to change about the way you've been subconsciously living.

Without being in full acceptance of all that you are, there will always be an element of shame. And shaming yourself into changing can only be sustained through shame. You don't want that. Authenticity is your goal. That means that you self-compassion your way through your change.

When you don't know who you are or, worse, when you don't accept who you are, you simply don't seek change for yourself. You seek change in order to alter the way that others see you because you are seeking *their* acceptance, because their acceptance feels better than your own acceptance. For example, if you're in a relationship and you constantly hear comments such as "you're too sensitive," you might doubt your own perception of events just to become less sensitive and to please your partner. Or if you receive comments on the way you dress (that it's too revealing, not revealing enough, too daring, not daring enough, and so on), you eventually change the way you dress to fit the other person's preference for you. Then you lose your own preferences, and the changes you make are inauthentic. What's more, inauthentic change is unreliable. It's easy for someone else to keep changing the milepost so that you are perpetually running to keep up. This gets you even further from knowing what you really want for yourself.

Do you see how dangerous that is?

Now let me remind you of something. If you are still working on accepting yourself and becoming aware of what made you who you are today, you don't have to wait for radical self-acceptance before you begin to change. You can be building that foundation within yourself while you are making the changes you need to make. As long as these changes are the result of trusting yourself, taking risks that you know are leading you closer to discovering your authentic self will actually serve the purpose of being in full self-acceptance and self-awareness.

Last week, a woman, Tina, booked a session with me. I always ask people ahead of time what they are hoping for in our session, and her comment was, "I need to figure out who I am so I can figure out what I want to do with my life." Read that again because I know that's very heavy.

You don't have to figure yourself out before you figure out what you want to do with your life. Both can happen at the same time. When I first started writing in 2013, I did not see myself as a writer. I wrote because it was the only way for me to feel seen and heard. Did I know who I was then? Absolutely not. But it was writing, and all the contemplation and reflection that was involved, that pushed me to go inward and ask myself all the important questions. As I was figuring out who I was and what I believed, I was also figuring out what I want to do in life.

I told the same thing to Tina. She had been in an abusive marriage for more than ten years. She was physically disabled. And after she finally had the courage to end that marriage, move to a new place, and start a new life, she got a job at a grocery store. She told me that long before she got married, she was very passionate about holistic health and healing. She always wanted to put content into the world that would help people through holistic healing. She told me that every time she reached out to a company to help her start a business where she could do this, they would tell her that she had to figure out exactly what she wanted to do before they could help her.

So very frustrated, Tina told me, "I need to figure out who I am before I figure out what I want to do." I said to her, "Who you are is someone who is currently figuring out who you are. There is nothing wrong with that. In fact, investing time in doing things you believe you want to do will help you figure out who you are. For example, if you want to help people through holistic healing, one thing you can do is start by sharing your experience with holistic healing. You can start a TikTok or an Instagram account and start by sharing tips from your experience, and you never know where that may lead you. You might enjoy it so much that you want to put out more content. And some people might start asking you questions that you can also answer and get more of an idea where your work is needed. You might also do it for a while and realize, *Hey! That's not for me!* Either way, you are investing your time in taking risks for yourself. Imagine you're trying to figure out what ice cream flavor you like without tasting any flavors at all."

If you are in that same spot, just ask yourself, *What is one thing I can do right now to bring me closer to figuring out who I am while I do something that I have been wanting to do?*

4. Wanting to Belong

Oftentimes what stops us from changing is the fear of exclusion. One of the most ironic things about wanting to belong is that on our quest to belong, we end up excluding our authentic selves. The quest to *belong* somewhere is what leads us to *fit in* instead. We look at the environment in which we want to belong, study the requirements of belonging in it, and change ourselves to fit that mold. Though on the outside it may look like we belong to that environment or to that group, internally we feel excluded.

At the heart of exclusion is the pain of isolation. It is the pain of feeling as though you are alone on your journey. Or that you are not welcome in the world in which you felt welcome for so long. Once we attempt change, isolation alone can cause a relapse into our old patterns.

On your journey to living the life you want, you might have to be a pattern-breaker, a status-quo-disruptor, and a change-driver. For example, if you are part of a family where it is expected that you get married by a certain age and in certain traditional ways, and you choose differently for yourself, that threatens the status you hold within your family and, subsequently, your community. The isolation and shame you will experience is a big deterrent from change.

As difficult as it is to live in isolation, even if it's just in our minds, we have to be willing to see it as a necessary step for healing our understanding of who we are. We have to see it as a pathway to being able to choose who we want to be in our own lives.

Going through a period of isolation allows us to go inward and pushes our deepest pains to the surface. That allows us to spend time with them, with parts of ourselves we weren't aware of or that we kept pushing down out of fear of feeling them. Isolation means we have more time to ourselves, and that naturally causes us to face a whirl of thoughts and emotions that we didn't have time to deal with before. We have to see isolation as a necessary step in the process of learning that the conditional version of love we were taught is not authentic love. Though it may present itself as such, it's not. Authentic love is love for your authentic self, not the filtered, edited, living-in-survival-mode self.

Have you heard the saying "a divorced daughter is better than a dead daughter"? The fact that this saying is so widespread across cultures uncovers a deeper issue. Think of Sania Khan, the woman I spoke about in chapter 1. So many cultures thrive on enmeshment; there is no differentiation between the self and the other. One person's actions reflect on the whole family, and the family's reputation among others reflects on the individual. What that means is that there is immense pressure on individuals to uphold a certain standard of allegiance to the family that oftentimes comes at the cost of what the individual wants for themselves or what is in their best interest.

So, for example, if a woman decides to get a divorce, because of the negativity attached to the image of a divorced woman and her family, the family will do anything to deter her from going through with it. Sadly, this happens even if abuse is present in the relationship. The saying "a divorced daughter is better than a dead daughter" came about as an outcry to prevent the death of women by domestic violence. That such a quote exists just demonstrates how difficult change can be for individuals coming up against cultural beliefs and traditions. And sadly, if a woman does succeed in leaving on her own, often without the support of her family, she is treated as if she's brought shame to her family. Imagine the effect that has on a woman and her feeling of belonging.

That example is specific to women, but wanting to belong affects everyone. Men often get criticized for not being "manly enough" or for expressing emotion. And that translates to their direct and indirect exclusion within society. Think of the cultures that still heavily condemn homosexuality, and worse, cultures that kill those who are homosexual. The places in the world where these aren't issues anymore only got there because of the collective sacrifice over centuries of those who decided to live their authentic truth.

The ostracization that a person disrupting the status quo experiences is oftentimes the reason they choose the pain of continuing to be part of an environment that heavily conditions their belonging over the pain of the consequences of choosing to change. Because at least they belong somewhere. When attempting change threatens the status we hold as a member of a certain environment, we might be deterred from that change because we believe we are risking the loss of belonging. And we believe it is 100 percent our responsibility. But the true question is, "Are we risking true, authentic belonging; or are we risking belonging that is conditional on us abandoning ourselves?"

Yes, the previous examples talk about much more intense and difficult deterrents and obstacles to change, but it's the same issue at the core of any kind of environment in which we want to belong. Think, for example, of wanting to apply for a higher position in your company but being hyperaware that if you do that, you will be considered an outsider to your closest circle of colleagues because you no longer are on the job in the way they are. Or think of making the decision to move to a new country but realizing it means you won't have a base (family, community, support system, friends, and so on) that anchors you.

If the changes you believe you need to make for yourself are driven by wanting to belong, slow down. Your job in life is not to find the place where you belong. It is to discover who you are authentically and to live that authentic truth. When you do, belonging becomes a simple matter of honoring that authentic truth. You will not want to be in places where it is necessary to hide parts of yourself.

Isolation becomes a natural part of your healing journey because you know that you are experiencing it as a result of a choice you made for yourself, a choice that brings you closer to the life you want.

5. Resistance

Resistance might be due to any of the aforementioned elements that hinder change. The reason that I want to talk about it separately is, oftentimes, the first indication of a hindrance to change is feeling your body resisting doing what needs to be done to accomplish that change. It sometimes takes the form of procrastination, lack of energy, lack of motivation, or simply finding more comfort in your current situation. Let me explain.

Sometimes when there is a change you're contemplating, you find yourself clinging to what you want to let go of. If there is a job you want so badly to leave, you might find yourself trying to make it work just so that you don't have to leave. Now this is obviously done subconsciously. In his book *Necessary Endings: The Employees, Businesses, and Relationships That All of Us Have to Give Up in Order to Move Forward*, Henry Cloud says, "The fool tries to adjust the truth so he does not have to adjust to it." For example, when you want to end a friendship, you might find yourself putting out signals that your friend finally picks up and then asks if you're okay. Instead of being honest about no longer wanting to be friends, you make a gesture that shows that you very much want this friendship to continue. Don't tell me you've never done this with anyone at some point in your life. I've seen this referred to as fawning, which is a trauma response where you over-please and over-serve to avoid conflict at any cost. This doesn't mean that those things feel good to you. It could simply mean that this feels better than the awful feeling of displeasing someone.

Does that make sense?

Again, just like uncertainty, fear, wanting to belong, and lack of self-acceptance and self-awareness, resistance serves the purpose of keeping us in the familiar that is more comfortable than the perceived danger of the unfamiliar.

Once we tune into our body and ask why we are resisting change, the answer begins to reveal itself. Are you resisting because you are uncertain, afraid, wanting to belong, or feeling out of alignment with who you are?

Change requires real work. It requires a commitment to do what it takes to accomplish the change. Many of us will sit in a state of resistance because we know subconsciously that change will require moving in a direction opposite to the one in which we've been moving. We are creatures of habit. And even though the outcome of our efforts to change might be somewhat guaranteed, we resist having things go differently in our lives.

Think of a time in your life when you decided to make a change, whether it was beginning to eat healthier, moving to a new place, preparing to leave a relationship, or something else. Now think of the time when you started executing your plan. You may have started off strongly but, bit by bit, you fell back into the comfort of the initial situation you had going on. Remember, your body naturally resists what is unfamiliar to it, even when that unfamiliar is actually safe for you. Being safe and feeling safe are two different things.

Combatting resistance can be as simple as saying, "Oh, I see I am experiencing some resistance right now; it's a natural body response to change." Anticipating this natural reaction will help you use it to your advantage.

I'm sure you've heard "what you resist persists." We usually say that to deter ourselves from stopping a certain thought or feeling. The more you resist it, the more it demands to be seen and heard by you. Think of a time you decided to avoid texting someone. The harder you tried to avoid that, the harder it became to not text them. So, instead of focusing on avoiding what you don't want, focus on what you do want. One of the most important elements of change from chapter 1 is "to see change as a path to the life you want."

Let's try to use "what you resist persists" to our advantage. If what you are resisting is a change that you actually deeply want for yourself, the change will keep demanding that you embrace it. To get yourself from the point of resisting to doing the work, you have to sit with the change that's demanding to be done by your authentic self and figure out why you're resisting it.

Then you have to decide what you'll do. Are you going to pursue the change, or are you going to reject it? The worst thing is not deciding. The journey between where you are and where you want to be begins with a decision.

Back in 2015, when I enrolled in my doctorate program, I was excited by the idea that I would be done with school in 2018, at the age of twenty-eight. But life doesn't always happen as expected. For many reasons that were out of my control, I found myself taking multiple consecutive leaves after successfully finishing half the program. In 2020, after COVID hit, I found myself itching to rejoin the program because I didn't want to keep an unfinished story in my life. I loved my program. I love education. Because the research I was conducting had to do with making schools more inclusive of newcomers, there was a part of me that felt like I was not being fair to myself or to all the people I could be helping. So, after going through the process of applying again and asking professors to write me reference letters, I finally got my acceptance letter. I was so happy but at the same time worried because I knew the amount of work that was required of me. At that time, I was finalizing my most recent book, *Welcome Home*, and I had a lot going on in my life personally. But I made the decision that I deserved the investment of my own time in my future more than most of the things in which I was investing that were completely out of my control.

After rejoining the program, I was overwhelmed with the amount of work involved. Going back to becoming fluent in academic writing after writing in my own style was honestly one of the hardest things I've had to do in my entire life. My professor at the time even commented that I needed to remind myself that I was writing academically. I was so close at so many points to just withdrawing from the program because I felt like what it required of me was not something I had. I did have it, but I was so tired of constantly working that I felt there was no way I could gather the energy needed for this program. I would dread sitting down and getting work done, which made the part of getting the work done much harder. When you dread doing something, you already set it up for failure.

That right there was resistance. On a logical level, I decided to go back to the program because I wanted to finish what I started and to leave an impact in the world that would make a difference for so many. I had the time. I had the energy. But I felt that I just needed a break from the go-go-go lifestyle I had. Instead of giving myself breaks in between so that I would have energy to do the work, I just worried all the time.

I would hear my mind telling me, *Najwa, you've worked hard enough in your life. It's time for you to live and enjoy yourself. Instead of spending your weekend reading and writing and doing school work, you should be out living. Haven't you worked hard enough?* There were times when I'd listen to that voice and just take a break from my work to go out and enjoy myself. But there were other times when I was so aware of the resistance. I realized that what I had to do was admit to myself that this was hard. And that going back to school two years after I thought I would be done for good was hard. When that resistance first started, a task that should take me an hour or two would require the whole day because I was in this constant back and forth with my mind. But once I realized that the battle I was fighting was with myself, I brought myself back into alignment. I needed my body and my mind to be on the same page. Once they were, I started getting my tasks done efficiently. Something on which I would have invested days, because of all the time spent in fighting the work that I had to do, would take me hours to complete. I started doing much better with much less time spent on tasks because I wasn't wasting my energy fighting with myself.

To align my body with my mind, I had to give my body enough rest and not keep it in a state of exhaustion and depletion. So, I would divide my time among writing, school, rest, and life.

Your body always has its say in a choice. And sometimes weeks, months, or even years after your mind makes a choice, your body will align with it. And you must honor the fact that your body needs its time to redefine for itself what safety looks like. So, if you've logically made a decision for yourself but feel that you are struggling to get it done because every time you try, you relapse, be gentle with yourself. Show yourself some compassion. As long as you are doing your absolute best to follow through with that decision, then you are literally doing what you are able to do. Sometimes, you have to recognize, *This is what I've decided for myself. But I need some time to align my mind with my body. So, right now, I'm in between making the decision and executing the decision.*

There are many ways around resistance, but here is my recipe:

1. Acknowledge the change that you're attempting is hard, and that it will require an alteration in your daily routine.
2. Set time aside for the work that needs to be done, during which your focus will be 100 percent on the task at hand.
3. Don't spend the rest of your time outside of the task worrying about the work you have to do. When worry visits, remind yourself that now is not the time to be focused on that task.

4. Focus on the small change at hand. Big changes take multiple small changes.
5. Celebrate small victories.

Understanding the forces at work to stop you from change will facilitate pushing through the change. We, as humans, like to *know*. We like to know where we're headed. We like to know the outcome of our efforts. We like to know that we are on the right path. Fear of not making the right change might deter you from moving forward with it. The key is to trust yourself in leading that change and getting through it the same way you've trusted others in your life to decide for you. Conviction in your ability to get through the change, even if it might not go the way you wanted, is the magical ingredient that will guide you.

As you navigate the duration of the change, you are engaging in a process of self-discovery. You are learning more and more about yourself, including your fears, anxieties, and patterns of being, as well as the things that excite you, the things you are good at, and so on. One of the beautiful things about getting to know yourself is realizing all the places where you've been trying really hard to feel welcomed and the people who don't truly see or accept you as you are. The resistance you feel to making a change will become your ally once you understand that it's a natural reaction. Just like enduring increased resistance in any physical activity builds stronger muscles, making your way through resistance builds stronger inner leadership—a stronger you.

CHAPTER 3

Changes We Don't Choose

When a change that we don't want is thrown our way, the lack of choice is painful. How many times have you found yourself chasing after something or someone only because they were unattainable? Or because there were so many obstacles in the way? You might be doing it right now. Sometimes the illusion of choice that comes with acquiring something that is unattainable gives a false sense of inner leadership. The focus isn't on whether we actually *want* what we are going for but on how capable we are of getting it. After achieving what we once thought was unreachable, the elusive sense of choice can leave us wondering, *Why did I even go for this in the first place?*

Acknowledge that with any change that life throws your way, it's okay to feel blindsided. Separating the innate nature of how your body reacts to things you don't choose from what that change actually is will help you discern whether you are struggling with the change itself or with a deeper belief about powerlessness. Is the power to choose your priority? Is the loss of that power what you are actually struggling with? Do you have a fear that anything you don't actively choose makes you lose control and therefore you must reject it? Do you panic that things never work out the way you want? Take out your journal and reflect on this.

It can feel unfair when you are forced to face a change you didn't want or see coming. You might find yourself thinking, *Why me? Why now? I'm not ready for this.* All valid points. The goal isn't to tell yourself how you should or shouldn't feel about change, but to feel what you're feeling with compassion and understanding. When someone breaks up with you, you go through a period of shock. Before you can even assess whether this is a change you want, the fact that someone else made this decision for you might make you feel defeated, powerless, and unwanted. Those feelings are hard for anyone to deal with. Which is why you might find yourself spending a prolonged period of time in denial or just not wanting to deal with this change. You might judge yourself for the way that you deal with this or how long it takes for you to accept it and move on. In moments like this, remember that the judgmental voice isn't yours; it was internalized from your environment. There are enough people in this world who have judged you—make the decision to not be one of them. Your authentic self is your biggest ally, advocate, and friend. Spend more time giving yourself the compassion needed when life throws a curveball. If you did see it coming but didn't welcome it, give yourself the gift of sitting in those tough moments, allowing yourself to grieve the reality you thought you had. Let yourself feel the fear and uncertainty for what lies ahead.

Now, we will learn how to accept change that we didn't decide for ourselves. To go from our current reality, the one that may be desired or simply the "normal" to which we're accustomed, to another that feels new, unstable, uncertain, or even scary.

1. Practice Radical Acceptance

The response to any change that we don't choose should be the same: radical acceptance. Before you turn the page because you've heard this before and it didn't work for you, just read the next two paragraphs. Because, at first, radical acceptance didn't work for me either. I had heard this term often, and my understanding of it was that it meant to accept that the situation is what it is, that I can't change it, and to let go of what is out of my control. With that definition, I still had a hard time. I'd think, *But how do I just accept it? It's unfair! It's hard! It's constantly on my mind.*

The missing piece for me was always the acknowledgment that, for things to be fair or just or even okay, things *should* have been different. And it wasn't that I needed to get rid of that "should." It's that I needed to follow it with "but they were not." Do you see what that does? It acknowledges my longing for things to be different. And it acknowledges that they're not. I had always gotten stuck on the part where I had to accept what I didn't want. But I realized radical acceptance is about validating for myself that I want things to be different and making the decision to not invest my energy into changing what I have no control over.

Isn't that powerful? I mean, it instantly adjusted the way I felt about so many things in my life. It made me feel detached; not in a numb kind of way, but in a way no longer dependent on things to change for me to feel better about myself. And in that, there's the reassurance I am actively giving myself that I am okay and safe within the existence of this reality.

Radical acceptance simply means that you see reality as it is and accept it. Even if you thought things were different or wanted them to be different, you accept that they are what they are. And you let go of doing anything to try to change them back to what they were, even though you might really want to. The acceptance part doesn't necessarily mean you approve of reality. It just means that you see it as it is and don't live in denial of it.

I used to get stuck in denial any time an uninvited change came into my life. And let me tell you, there is no easier way out of experiencing pain than denial. But the numbing only worked for a short amount of time.

When I was twenty-two years old, shortly after graduating with a bachelor's in education, I took a job at a private school. It paid minimum wage. I took that job because I felt like a failure having graduated with a teaching degree and not having a teaching job. I also took it because I didn't want to take any more student loans to cover my master's program tuition. Because what they paid me wasn't enough to cover my tuition, my expenses, and my previous loan payments, I offered private tutoring lessons after school and on weekends, taught Arabic at Saturday school for high schoolers, and worked with my brothers at their car dealership doing paperwork—all while completing my master's and working full time.

The crazy thing is, at that time, I thought I wasn't doing enough.

One time (I can't believe I'm telling this story because it's so embarrassing—actually, it felt embarrassing at the time but now it's just hilarious.), after teaching a three-and-a-half-hour class at Saturday school, I headed to work at my brothers' dealership. Their offices were in a trailer that was elevated from the ground by a little bit less than a meter. I usually parked at the end of the trailer, where my oldest brother's office was. His name is Kamal, by the way. All I remember was that I was driving to get to work, and, all of a sudden, I felt myself crash right under Kamal's office. The whole front of my car, right up to the windshield, was under the trailer.

It's safe to say, I burst into tears because I couldn't believe I did something like that. *It probably will cost my brothers so much to fix it. What if I hurt someone?* To be quite honest, I don't think I was crying because of any of that. I think I was crying because I was exhausted. I was exhausted from running a race that I felt had no finish line. All I was concerned with was staying on track. Because there was no other option. Falling off track was so much worse than not being on the track altogether. What if I had stopped tutoring seven days a week and just focused on a full-time job and full-time school? Then I wouldn't be able to afford school, which I chose to pay for out of my own pocket. My focus was completely on reaching certain milestones in life, again, indoctrinated within me by the environment that raised me and the one that surrounded me (no, not just my family, because they were affected by that same environment I was affected by). I needed to go as far through school as I possibly could, at the youngest age possible. I needed to be debt-free ASAP. I needed to become the best teacher I could become as fast as possible. But according to whom?

According to yours truly.

Maybe doing all of this would make my parents proud of me. Maybe doing all of this would make others say, "Wow, you're doing all of that??!!" Maybe that would make me feel good about myself. And, most sadly, maybe doing all of this would fill the emptiness I felt inside. Fix the unlovableness (Is that even a word?) I felt inside. Resolve the *something must be wrong with me to feel this desperate need for love* I felt inside. Maybe doing all of that would fill this desperate need to be seen and. . . .

Actually, I don't want to rush that sentence. Because I use this phrase—need to be seen—often, and I haven't really taken the time to discuss it. Ah, tears come to my eyes as I write that. All that time, I thought that being seen was being recognized for my accomplishments, that everything I did was seen as an indication that I was worthy. That my drive and ambition would be an indication that I was worthy of earning someone's "I'm so proud of you." But the truth was, I just wanted to be seen as worthy without all of that. I didn't want to be working so hard to prove that I'm one of the good ones. That I am enough. That I am deserving of being loved by someone. Anyone.

As my car was still under Kamal's office, I was still quietly, but internally very loudly, crying my heart out. I was tired of running this race. What a wake-up call that was.

That wake-up call was so powerful, in fact, that I am baffled when I look back at how it still managed to not wake me up. Because I continued on that racetrack. Until months later, when I woke up one morning to excruciating abdominal pain. At first, I thought it was something I ate. But as the day went on, it got worse and worse. And before you assume I didn't take that day off work . . . you're right. I obviously didn't. I spent the day standing in front of my students feeling like I could faint any moment. I knew something was very wrong.

That pain persisted for a few days. I made an appointment with my family doctor, who immediately sent me for a bunch of procedures. He said he could tell something was off from my bloodwork, that the white blood cell count was abnormally high. A few days later, for a whole day, I was at a hospital where I had a colonoscopy scheduled. The preparation for the procedure and the procedure itself took hours. And because the sedative was so powerful, I was asleep for a few hours afterward. And I'll never forget this moment. As soon as I opened my eyes, this old, very much in a rush, doctor walked in and started speaking to my mom who was sitting right next to me. He said, "She has Crohn's disease. It was very obvious. I didn't even have to wait for the results of the biopsy. She's in a state of active inflammation right now, so you need to pick up these medicines, and she needs to go on them immediately."

We picked up the prescriptions on our way home, and I immediately started taking them. I didn't even look at the list of side effects. But you better believe that I had to once I started experiencing the absolute worst of them—sleepless nights where my head, hands, and feet would feel like they were on fire; crippling anxiety and feelings of doom about life and everything in it; having no appetite but somehow gaining weight in my face. My cheeks got so big, I remember thinking my face looked like that of a chipmunk . . . cute, yes, but very unlike how I'd always known my face to be. I know now it's because the doctor had me on steroids.

This change that I had no control over (Crohn's is half genetic, half environmental from what my doctor explained to me) put a halt to that race I was running. When I didn't listen to the car wake-up call, my body said, *I'll give you a crash that'll wake you up.*

I quit my job at that private school at the end of the school year and thankfully completed my master's shortly after. So that part was good. But you know what wasn't? The fact that I wanted to continue living my life as if I didn't have Crohn's and as if all the side effects of the medications were not there. I was living in denial. I would feel myself getting angry every time I would think of the fact that I have Crohn's, but I would push that anger inside because "I wasn't someone who got angry."

It wasn't until I sat down with myself and considered, *I really don't want to have Crohn's. But I have it. And that's a fact I literally cannot change. If it were up to me, I would erase it from my body, but I don't have that kind of power. What I have power over is figuring out what the best way to nourish my body is given the situation it's in and do my best to give it what it needs.*

The sad reality was that my body was already in conflict with itself. If you don't know this, Crohn's is an autoimmune disease. Your body is literally fighting an infection inside of itself, created by itself. So, my body was at war with itself. And I was at war with my body.

What I needed to do was befriend my body so that I could at least lessen its suffering . . . my suffering.

Does that example of radical acceptance make sense now? The formula for radical acceptance is this:

1. I acknowledge that I want this reality to be different.
2. I acknowledge that it's not different.
3. I accept this reality is what it is.
4. I choose to not allow what I cannot control to control me.

This works for any change over which we have no control. Even though I can't walk through examples of every possible change that happens to us in this chapter, remember this works for other changes as well, like losing a job or even aging.

Now I have another story to share with you, and there's no easy way to transition into something like this, but here it is.

2. Grieve

When I first got the news that my grandma passed away, I cried like a baby. I fell to my knees and cried for hours. I couldn't believe it. I couldn't imagine that there was no more speaking to her, ever. I couldn't imagine that the next time I'd go to Lebanon, she wouldn't be there.

I couldn't imagine that there would never be another time that I'd walk through the door and see her sitting in the exact same spot, about a half a meter away from the edge of the couch she always sat on.

My memories of her started racing through my mind, how she'd cradle my head in her lap and whisper words of love and protection as she stroked my hair and face and shoulders. How she'd always ask me if I was hungry. How she'd go to the back room and return with a plate of my favorite fruits that she'd set aside just for me. I was recalling those memories and fighting away the possibility that her death was true. Every time I'd remember getting that phone call and being told, "I'm sorry. She's gone," every fiber in my body would push that moment away. I wanted to erase it. I wanted to reverse time to the moment right before, when her being gone was not part of reality. Because now my reality will never be the same. Life without her will never be the same as life with her. Just knowing that she was there to pick up the phone when I called was a much better reality to live in than one where I could never hear her voice again. Or see her.

I just wasn't ready.

The truth is, I never wanted to be ready for something like that.

Grief is like a big tide that pulls you in and, for a moment, you feel like you and this reality cannot coexist, that accepting that loss is simply out of the picture. It's impossible. A part of you feels like accepting it will make it real. You feel like you're going to drown in the dark ocean that this tide is pulling you into. So, every part of you is fighting to go back to the place where you didn't feel this way. And the more you fight, the harder it becomes to get back to the surface.

The real answer is to just let the tide take you wherever it takes you. If it wants to take you to a place where you live in the memories as if they are happening right now, let it. If it wants to take you to the place where you're sad because you're missing the memories, let it. If it wants to take you to a place where you imagine how you're going to honor them throughout your life, let it. I know it's scary to do that because there is 0 percent of you that wants to live in a world where the only way to have that person there is by honoring them instead of seeing them, hearing them, or holding them. If you find yourself resisting that place, know there is no judgment for that. It's not wrong to have a hard time accepting loss. Even the period of time when you're in denial of their loss is an expression of love toward them.

Remember the lady who told my grandpa that his crying over my grandma somehow symbolized his lack of gratitude to God and acceptance of God's will? Be careful to not fall into that trap. Don't allow anyone to dictate how long or short your grief should last. Love doesn't work that way, and life doesn't work that way. You may grieve this person for the rest of your life. And that's okay.

When you run away from grief, you push the parameters of what you need to heal. You create a bigger circle of grief around you. Because what you're running away from is within you. It's not like there's any place in this world you could go where the reality of the loss of someone just doesn't exist. To get to a place where you can escape the acceptance of that reality, you take on behaviors that temporarily distract you from that reality. That's why you feel numb by spending extra time at work, creating to-do lists for all the things you feel you need to do to get your life in order, making sure you always have plans so you feel like you know what you're doing, and so on. Some of us go numb by using alcohol and drugs. Some of us go numb by seeking comfort in people. Some of us go numb by pushing away every person who loves us. We obviously don't do this out of not wanting love, but out of fear that they will truly see us and our pain. Because when we are seen for who we are, there is the potential that the ugly parts of ourselves are exposed too. And instead of focusing on shining all the other parts that need to feel seen by and connected to others, we protect the whole of ourselves from being seen altogether. It just feels safer to do so.

Grief doesn't wait for the right time to visit us. It comes when it comes, and it's our choice to welcome it or not. But as long as we don't welcome it, it will continue to knock until it is able to walk in, sit with us for a while, and then perhaps move into another room in our home. Then it might move out and visit every so often. But by not allowing it in, we are building a protective shield that hinders our acceptance of reality.

When it comes to grief for the loss of a person through death, here is a list of things I recommend:

1. Be sad.
2. Allow yourself to say all the things you are afraid to say. *I wish I had spent more time with them. I wish I had handled that situation differently. I wish I had told them I love them one last time.*
3. Say it all and cry it out if you need to.
4. Take the time you need to process.
5. Take the soul space you need to hold the grief for them.
6. Let that big gaping valley of love you have for them go toward them. Imagine them receiving it. Oftentimes it hurts to have love that has nowhere to go.

I've heard people talk about death in a way that expresses anger toward the one who died. Maybe there was some kind of unfinished business. That usually manifests itself as anger. Because there is lack of closure. Maybe there is something the griever was waiting to have acknowledged or an apology that never came. Whatever the case may be for you—perhaps you don't feel their death affected you the way it affected others around you, or you feel like it is a relief—just understand that death doesn't affect us all in the same way. And that's okay. You know your story and what you've been through more than anyone else does.

This brings me to a different kind of grief, one that is seemingly reversible—the end of a relationship. Perhaps that grief, in many ways, doesn't differ from the grief of losing someone; the shock of going from them being in our lives to them no longer being there, the part where we don't want to accept that this is true, the part where we struggle with going to places that remind us of them, and so on. But overall it is a different kind of grief, one that begs the question: "Why is someone's choice to no longer be part of my life so painful?"

Grieving the loss of someone through death is obviously different than grieving the loss of someone who is still alive. Because when they are alive, we have to deal with the reality that they are there, that we can realistically speak to them, hear their voice again, see their face again, and hold them again, but either they or we are choosing not to. It really is a different kind of grief. Losing someone through death often makes one thing clear to us—sometimes we spend more time hurting over someone who chose not to be with us than someone who we lost through death. And we have a harder time accepting loss of someone in life than in death. It's not always an indication of how much love we have for the person we lost. We can love someone we lose through death a lot more than we love someone we lose in life but still spend more time grieving the latter. Maybe death comes with an inherent tendency for acceptance because it's one of the very few constants in life.

This awareness shook me. I obviously love my grandma a lot more than I love any of my friends or anyone with whom I'd ever been in a relationship. A few days after my grandma died, in thinking about relationships, friendships, and dreams, I knew in my heart that her death was so much bigger and tougher than any other kind of loss I had endured in my life or any kind of loss I could endure in my life. It really put things into perspective. I went through days where I didn't answer my messages or calls or emails. I fell off the schedule I had for working on this book and then continuing to promote my other books—all those things that seemed to be so important and difficult to abandon became things that I saw very clearly could be stopped for a while without the world coming to an end.

I had a friend who texted me a couple of days after my grandma died, without knowing that she had passed, and a few days after the first message, she sent me another one complaining that I hadn't responded. Even seeing that woke me up to reconsidering the kinds of friendships I have and the kinds of relationships I have with everyone around me.

Because as much as I have become a person who knows her

worth and value, who knows how to draw boundaries and not allow what others think of me to rule my life, I still managed to hold on to relationships from the past that were there long enough to continue existing. And it's not like they were relationships that were present in my everyday life. They were just people with whom I interacted every once in a while and people who I was there for only occasionally. There was never a big reason for me to reconsider my relationships with those people. Nothing bad happened, but also nothing good. The relationships felt like placeholders and time fillers. I had continued being my kind, present self with people who only accepted me as long as I was that kind, always available me. I will address this further in chapter 5.

A few days after my grandma died, as I was crying myself to sleep, I could feel her arms around me. I went back to being a little kid running to her and laying the weight of my little body on her. The love she had for me was so pure and healing. I couldn't believe that I spent so much time of my life being sad over people who decided to walk out of my life when I was so blessed to have this pure love from my grandma. With people who chose to leave, what was I sad about? Their love never felt like love once their true colors started showing. They left me feeling as though I didn't deserve their love. How could I have wasted so much of my time grieving their loss while I could've spent that time reveling in this pure love I had?

I was being so hard on myself, wishing I'd spent less time dwelling on love I didn't have and more time on love I did, love that meant so much more. And that's when it dawned on me that sometimes, someone's choice to no longer be with us is what hurts, not the love we have for them, and definitely not that their love is no longer there. It was their choice to leave us when they had a choice to stay. It's what that choice tells us about our worth. And it's okay if it hurts that much. Yes, it's true that not all relationships end on bad terms. Some end with lingering love from both sides. But the fact that someone chooses to no longer be with us despite their love for us is also hurtful. It sends the message that we are not worth their sacrifice. As different as both types of loss are, the pain of losing love is all the same at the end. The bond that was there broke. And that hurts.

When it comes to the end of a relationship of any kind, whether it was an end we wanted or not, it causes change in our lives. The bond that tied us to them in some way has been severed, and that may propel us in a direction where we feel we've lost stability. That's where resilience comes in.

3. Develop Resilience through Self-Compassion

What often keeps us stuck in the pain caused by changes that happen to us and interferes with our ability to get unstuck is a lack of compassion. Specifically, a lack of self-compassion. Yes, compassion from others helps, but no amount of compassion from others can compensate for the compassion we need from ourselves.

Think of the last time something happened to you and no amount of reassurance from those you love and trust helped you feel better. That's because when rain falls on a water-resistant fabric, it trickles right off. When compassion falls on someone who wholeheartedly does not believe they deserve compassion, that compassion goes in one ear and out the other. If you whole-heartedly believe you don't deserve compassion, it's because shame has been an occupant inside of you for so long that it's hard for you to separate yourself from it. It's driving you.

Self-compassion is the answer. Instead of immediately going to shame, take a detour around the self-judgment road and try the self-compassion road instead. On the self-compassion road, you will sit with yourself and aim to understand how you feel instead of judging yourself.

Begin by asking yourself, *Is what I went through actually shameful? Or is it an experience that I am labeling as shameful as a result of my conditioning* [by family, community, partner, and so on]*?* You know the answer.

I understand how hard it is to shake years of conditioning off your heart and soul. I am still in the process of doing that myself. You don't undo that overnight. You undo bit by bit. Unlearn bit by bit. Redefine bit by bit. As much as you want to just be free of that conditioning, the solution is not to run away from it but to face it head on. When you run away from something, anything, you give it the power of always having the potential to catch up to you. And when it does, if you haven't taken the time to develop the tools to face it, it will dig its claws into you even harder than it did before. It also means that you will always be running. And that's exhausting.

When you find yourself experiencing shame, take a moment to ask yourself where it's coming from. Dismantling years of conditioning is a messy process that involves a whole lot of self-compassion (walking in your own shoes), self-forgiveness (forgiving yourself for what you did when you were living in survival mode), and self-love (being your own best friend and advocate). This is how you develop resilience.

I used to think that resilience had to do with snapping back into the reality that existed before the event that changed things for me. I realize now it has nothing to do with snapping back into any kind of reality that existed before. Rather it has to do with snapping forward into your authentic self and finding safety in being who you are and living as you are. It has to do with having the trust in yourself that you'll get through anything to the best of your ability. And before you panic and say, *But I don't know who I am!* remember that the journey back to yourself requires discovering your authentic self that is free of the conditioning that brought you to this point in your life. Moments when you find yourself falling into self-judgments are perfect opportunities for you to learn who you actually are, free of who you were taught you were: *How do I feel?* versus *How have I been conditioned to feel?*

Through discovering your authentic self that is free of conditioning, you gain skills and tools to assist with showing your authentic self the compassion it needs as you are shedding layers of conditioning, breaking patterns from which you operated for years, and redefining who you are. I talk about this process of discovery in my last book, *Welcome Home.*

When we hear that someone went through a life-changing event, we might think that the intensity of the event itself is what defines the strength of the person who went through it. News flash: It's not the event itself. It's how it was experienced by a person in the moment. And what it changed inside of them. This is in no way intended to judge anyone for how they dealt with their specific trauma or to compare traumas. A trauma is specific to the person who experienced it. And some traumas rob us of certain parts of ourselves that take time to come back, if they ever come back. Sometimes, we are just left with spaces inside of us that are empty. It might take years before we feel those parts starting to fill up again. For example, if an event left someone with the trauma of feeling like they can't trust anyone but themselves, that could leave them with years of keeping closed the parts of themselves that really want to open up.

Resilience is taking the whole of who you are and everything that contributed to your current reality and radically accepting it all by acknowledging, *I, with every part of who I am, and with everything that happened to me, am worthy. I lead the path ahead for myself with compassion toward my current self and my past self that was conditioned to believe that I can only be loved when I fit certain molds and follow certain rules.* When you tie this to the life you want to live (as we discussed in chapter 1), resilience (being able to come back to yourself) becomes natural to you.

4. Go Inward

When something in your life ends and it feels like the end of your life, take it as an invitation to shed the old you, the old life, and begin a new one that includes the change that happened.

Let's take the example of someone ending a relationship with you. Here is an example of going inward. You can adapt the following steps to any other situation where an unwanted ending is thrust upon you.

1. Pause. Acknowledge the overwhelm and confusion. It is so common for us to immediately panic and get overwhelmed with our feelings of sadness in the moment. We start asking questions. There's a part of us that doesn't believe they mean what they're saying, because when we think back to all the moments we shared with them, where they were 1,000 percent certain about us, those moments and this current moment do not add up. There's a lot of confusion. Maybe there were conversations where the two of you decided that you would make this work. Maybe you shared a really beautiful moment recently.

2. Process what just happened. All in all, it is absolutely essential that you take a moment to tell yourself you need to process what you just heard. And that you need to think about it. Now I know many of you are thinking, *That breakup already happened. I already freaked out and*

questioned them and said a few things that, in retrospect, I regret saying. I accused them of things. I cried like a baby and made myself look weak.

3. Stop judging yourself. Look at the facts. Remember that when a relationship is the right one for you, no amount of reacting or overreacting will break it. Relationships that are good for you are not ones fragile enough to be broken by the way you reacted in the moment to a really painful event. Plus, if you overreacted when someone you deeply love decided they no longer want to be with you, how is that overreaction the reason that they don't want to be with you? They already made that decision before they came to you with it.

4. Be still and silent. It's important that you take the time to let that moment sink in, take some time before you respond, and take some time to figure out how you feel about the relationship.

5. Own your story. Every person's story is different. Maybe this person broke up with you at the most unexpected time. If that's the case, then this breakup will shake everything that you thought was real and true. It might cause you to have a mini identity crisis because you will find yourself going over every detail wondering what you missed and what you had a gut feeling about but were assured by them wasn't true. Maybe they even reassured you when you worried that they no longer wanted this relationship. Basically, you might feel extremely

confused and wonder how much you can actually trust your own judgment. Regardless of whether you saw this breakup coming or not, you need to take some time to process, reflect, and see how you feel about all of it. This will also depend on the length of this relationship. Be compassionate with yourself accordingly.

6. Decide. Ask yourself: *What do I want?* Since this is a decision that someone else made, reflect on what your decision would have been had you taken the time to decide what you want. Maybe this relationship wasn't good for you. Maybe it was one that you struggled very much with and were unhappy in. But there was always a part of you that felt either stuck or just wanted it to work. Sometimes the only reason you're holding on to a relationship is because of how good it was before. That's an especially hard experience because it sets the benchmark in your mind for how good it can be. And you think, *If they were able to be that good to me before, and if our relationship was that good before, then it has the potential to be that way again.* So, you're essentially basing how much you want it to work on how good it was or could be in the future, but not on how it makes you feel now. And that could speak to much deeper issues you have that must be addressed by you.

7. Do the work. This is the part where you take action to move toward a life where you've radically accepted the change.

But before we move onto the next chapter, I want to discuss how what you experience is not necessarily *about* your situation.

5. Don't Take Things Personally

Not everything that happens, happens *to* you. Sometimes it just happens, and you are affected by it. This is a good mindset to have when you struggle with thinking, *Why did this happen to me?* Do some things happen directly to you? Yes. Like getting fired from a job because of your performance or getting broken up with or getting a disease, and so on. In instances like this, it helps to remember that those experiences don't have to define you. They don't have to mean something about you. That's the only way through.

When a change happens in your life that you have no control over, it's easy to speak to yourself in a way that intensifies the pain more than its inherent intensity. So, instead of feeling the pain of that one event that happened, you feel the pain of the bigger question: *Why did this happen to me?* That's literally what it means to take it personally. You make what happened *to* you mean something *about* you, or that you deserved it happening to you. Maybe it just happened because someone else decided to do it. Maybe it happened because you did something that pushed it to happen. I mean this in the most non-victim-blaming way possible. But knowing that your actions have consequences pushes you to take accountability instead of plunging you into shame. And maybe what taking accountability looks like is learning to set your own boundaries. Maybe it's about learning what it is that has gotten you to a point in your life where you would allow a certain kind of behavior that caused you that kind of pain. Maybe it's about unlocking a certain potential that you've always been scared to explore. And maybe it's redirecting you away from something that in the long run is not good for you. By the same token, maybe it's directing you toward something that is good for you in the long run.

I also have to say this. I'm sure you've heard some spiritual guru at some point tell you that things don't happen *to* you, but they happen *for* you. If you subscribe to that way of thinking, there is no judgment. But I personally can never say that my Crohn's, for example, happened for me. Or that the death of my grandma happened for me. I can never tell someone who survived sexual assault that it happened for them. Things can happen *to* you and not *for* you at the same time. Things can happen to you and not define you at the same time. You can't control what life, or people, bring your way sometimes. What you can control is how you move forward from that and how you detach who you are from what happened to you.

CHAPTER 4

Changes We Choose

So you've made a decision to change something in your life. Now the hard part—actually going through with it. Take a moment to tune in to your body. What sensations do you feel as you think about making the change? Do you feel excited? Scared? Paralyzed with fear? Identify what you're experiencing. If you need to, grab a pen and paper to write it out. I can't remember a time in my life when I chose an important change that I didn't feel some part of my body wanting to run back in the direction of what I was trying to move away from. Do you relate to that? I used to perceive that as a possible sign from the universe that I needed to stay where I was. Now, I see it as my body's fear of letting go of the familiarity it knew for so long.

When I decided to embrace my own definition of what it means to be a woman, separate from what I was taught growing up, I focused on the consequences I would face as a result of the changes I would need to make, as opposed to being excited about the freedom I was giving myself to embrace the life I knew I wanted to live. I recognized that the comfort I felt in the old definition I was taught had nothing to do with my conviction that such a definition was okay. It had everything to do with the validation of those who taught me that definition. I wanted to please them. And what felt off about wanting to change was feeling that I was displeasing and disappointing those who wanted me to be a certain way. Can you relate to this?

Maybe what you are hoping for in this chapter is a step-by-step process for making your change. And you'll get that. But it's not the process you might be expecting. Before we talk about the *how* of change, I want you to ask yourself about the *why* of change.

Think of the change you are contemplating. Did you make this decision based on what *you* want, or did you make it based on what you *think* you want? I based many decisions on what I was taught my life needed to be for it to be considered successful. The simple thought that I could have a say in what I wanted for myself didn't even cross my mind. I was a follower—a great one, if I may add. I mean, if there was an award for the most perfect rule-follower, I would win it and hang it next to my university degrees.

Back when I was applying for university programs, I really wanted to do something related to social studies. I was and still am fascinated with how people think and why they behave in the ways they do. The university application allowed me to apply to three different programs. Knowing my dad wanted me to be a dentist, I had to apply to science. The other program I selected was social studies. I don't remember the third. The first acceptance letter I got was the social studies one. I was so happy. My dad definitely wasn't. He said he wasn't surprised I got accepted because I'm smart and can get into any program I want but that social studies would get me nowhere in life. To be a dentist, I needed to get into the science program. I immediately understood that the social studies program was not an option. Part of me honestly wished that my science application would be rejected. That was a moment in my life when I was willing to sacrifice what I really wanted to do in order to appease my need for acceptance. I remember also applying to the science program at a university that was a couple hours away from home and it was a hard no from my dad. Moving away at seventeen? Was I crazy? It didn't matter that I was accepted. It wasn't even seen as good news. I actually think I got in trouble for attempting to apply to a university so far away.

So I went into science at the local university and hated my life for the next few years. Even though I didn't enjoy science at all, I still had the goal of becoming a dentist. I beat myself up over not getting good grades and internalized it to mean that I wasn't studying hard enough even though I spent every waking moment studying. I was going after something I thought I wanted based on someone else's wants for me. And to meet their expectations, I had to convince myself their goals for me were my own.

Do you have goals in your life that you have based on what you've been taught your life needs to be? What would happen if you wrote down each of those goals and asked yourself, *Do I want this?* If your answer is "yes," ask yourself, *Why do I want this?* If the answer to your "why" is based on others' opinions about you or your goal, it's not an authentic goal to you.

I will tell you now, I will not coach you through a change that isn't authentic to you. My ultimate goal with this book, and with any book I write, is to transform your life into one that is led by authenticity. It is not my place to tell you what change is right or wrong for you. It is *your* place to tell yourself that. It's one thing to take people's input, advice, or feedback on the change you want and another thing to seek their approval or acceptance as essential to your moving forward with the change.

Today, I can proudly say I'm a recovering rule-follower turned into practicing rule-breaker. Ultimately, my goal is to become a rule-setter for myself. It's my hope that you will walk your own journey from follower to leader.

In the last chapter, we talked about changes that happen in our lives, ones we haven't chosen. Now we will talk about being intentional with change. You'll learn "how can I go from my current reality to my desired reality?" And the key word is *my*.

You don't need me to tell you that not all change is the same. Changing your wardrobe might not be as hard as, say, changing your program in school, or deciding you don't want to do school at all. Or it might be, based on your own circumstances. Own that. Don't let anyone tell you how hard or easy a change should be for you. You are the only one who knows it.

1. Become a Person of Choice

Of course, life will happen, and at times you'll have to grieve and accept changes. But there are changes that you are in control of. If you want to build an authentic life, you need to see your-self as the person who makes changes in your own life.

I am now thirty-two. I have my own apartment. I dress the way I like. I travel to the places I want. And I spend my time doing the work I love: this.

But let's go back five years. I was twenty-seven. I was living with my parents. I wore the hijab. I had a strict schedule of work, school, and teaching. And I only traveled for work, when it was necessary. Right now, I am experiencing the most peace I've ever experienced in my life.

When I was twenty-seven, I was experiencing the worst tur-moil I'd ever experienced in my life. Why? Because I was not living my life for myself. I was living it for everyone else.

When I was twenty-five years old, I was accepted into the Doctorate in Education program at the university I had attended since I was seventeen. Before that, at twenty-three, I graduated from a master's program in education. And before that, I gradu-ated with a bachelor's in education. And before that, I graduated with a bachelor's in science. Back then, I would have insisted that those were things I wanted, those were things I chose, but the truth was, I made those decisions in order to please my par-ents. What drove those decisions wasn't me taking ownership over my life. I wanted to please my parents so that I could be pleased with myself.

I started writing when I was twenty-three years old, during the toughest year of my life. Remember the car-crash story from chapter 3? It was that year. I was doing way too much. Yet every single day when I came home after long hours of teaching, working at my brothers' car dealership, and knowing that I had schoolwork or class in the evening, I sat down at the kitchen table with the din of my parents, sister-in-law, and the kids all around the house. I don't know how, but I managed to drown out the noise and let my heart spill onto paper. Doing that was not intentional. It wasn't something that I woke up every morning promising myself to do. It felt like something I had to do to keep going. That hour or two I spent every day writing down my thoughts and feelings was the only thing I was genuinely doing for myself. That was the only thing that gave me any form of relief. It was what I looked forward to every single day and what I felt sad leaving behind when I had to do all the other things on my list.

Thankfully, it was that pull, that craving, that got me to where I am today. By "where I am today," I mean that I am a person of choice. Writing gave me time to go inward. It gave me permission to have my own opinions on . . . everything. The practice of pausing to write every day prompted me to ask myself the questions that I wished those around me would ask: How are you today? How are you feeling? What's going through your mind? How did X person treating you in a certain way make you feel? What's your opinion on that topic you learned about earlier today? And so on. Writing gave me permission to be the most powerful part in the equation of my life. Not only did it empower me to see myself as an integral element in my life, but it gave me eternal validation that I am the writer of the script of my own life. I am now a person who values my peace over the opinions of others, no matter who they are. And when I say that I value my peace over the opinion of others, I'm not just talking about the negative opinions of others. I'm also talking about their approval.

I had been moving forward with school and exhausting myself because I was seeking my parents' positive opinion. And it's not that their opinion of me was a negative one. I just never received praise or compliments or positive words of affirmation for anything I did. I can confidently say my parents didn't do this with the intention of hurting my self-esteem or hurting me or making me feel unworthy. It's just how they were raised. But I am at a point now where I can separate their reality from my right to have experienced mine and been affected by mine the way that I was.

In working with my therapist, I learned that I could walk in someone else's story without leaving my own story. I worked so hard to become someone who they would be proud of.

Ah. This is the beauty of putting words to paper. Right now, you can't see the tears streaming down my face as I write this. Even with my current level of conviction and self-awareness, I still sometimes grieve my past self. I still have moments when I want so badly to go to my younger self and give her a hug and tell her that I'm proud of her. And that she didn't have to work so hard to feel loved and validated.

So now I am at a point in my life where I do my absolute best not to be led by my desire for anyone's validation. And I do my best not to be deterred from doing anything because it might cause a negative perception of me in someone else's eyes. Now, I value the desires of my authentic self over seeking validation or avoiding judgment from others. That's what it means to be a person of choice.

When I look at the choices I made in the past, I know they weren't choices I made for myself. They were choices I made for everyone else. It was only once I started to make choices for myself and be honest about the intention behind each choice that I began living a life of inner peace.

Start by reflecting on the intention behind minor everyday choices, like deciding what to eat. Reflect on who you're making that decision for—it might be a real eye-opener. Start in the morning with the clothing you put on, the makeup you wear, or the texts you send. Remember Veronica from chapter 1? The woman who said, "I didn't have a breakdown! I had a break-through?!" A big part of her breakthrough was learning her taste in music. She told me she had no idea what she liked. She just liked what he liked. Because that's all she gave herself per-mission to do. She was so consumed with molding to fit *him* so that maybe he would see her as worthy of love. It was the same with food. She cooked or ordered what was desired by everyone else, her kids included.

Next, think of the moments when you say things like, *I have to do this. I have no choice.* For example, *I'm in a toxic relationship so I have to leave* or *I'm in a job that doesn't pay me enough so I have to look for something else.* When people would say to me,

"You are so brave!" or "You're an inspiration for living your life the way you want," I'd think, *I don't see it that way. I see it as I had no choice.* But the truth is, I did have a choice. Even though these are choices I'm proud of, at the time, it was still easier to not take full responsibility for my choices and instead give power to everyone and everything around me for the changes I made. So instead of saying, "I chose to cut this person out of my life because their presence was toxic to my well-being," I'd say, "I had to cut this person out of my life because their presence was toxic to my well-being." Saying "I had to" took away from my agency, from my ability to give myself permission to decide for myself. It's the same thing when we say things like, "I have to put up with this toxic work environment or with my boss's dry jokes, because I need this job." We can believe that we have no choice, but in reality, we do. Taking charge of your life in a way that owns up to your decisions is empowering: "I choose to navigate my way through this toxic work environment, or to humor my boss when they try to be funny, because I need this job." Do you see the difference between saying "I choose to" versus "I have to"?

Sometimes you make a decision to run away from a bad situation. Those are still decisions that you should own. Because you shortchange your power if you just think that you're doing what you have to do. Owning that you made a good decision to get out of something bad builds the muscle of choice and builds your self-perception as a person of choice.

Perhaps it is better to think of these types of changes as a way *toward* instead of a way *out of* something. You are not running away out of fear, simply because staying put is unfathomable, but running toward something that you want. Fix your focus on what's coming instead of what you're leaving. To help with this, you can write down exactly what you're hoping would come into your life. Let's say you are leaving a partner who never prioritized you. Instead of focusing on avoiding a partner who does the same in the future, focus on visualizing having a partner who prioritizes you. This applies to change in any area of your life.

And maybe instead of running away from something you want to change, you could try walking. You could try to see the journey as one of small changes that will lead you to a bigger change. This doesn't mean that you escape or reject your present. It means that you stop arguing with your reality and dwelling on how unfair it is or how it should be different. It means that you fully and radically accept that it is what it is, that you can't change it, and that you want something different. It requires time. It requires patience with yourself, compassion with yourself, and, most important, trust in yourself.

So the first step in making a change is making sure that this choice is for you. For your authentic self. For your authentic life. Make sure that this is a choice *you* are making. Here is a list of questions that will guide you.

1. What's the change you've decided to make?
2. Why did you decide to make this change?

    a. Is this change based on what you want?

       i. If yes, go ahead.

      ii. If no, ask yourself: Where did the need for this change come from?

  3. Redirect back to yourself and make the choice *you* want.

This leads to the next important part of making change in your life.

2. Know Who You Are

When you make decisions for your life that are based on something other than the truth of who you are, an identity crisis is inevitable. It might not happen immediately, but it will manifest at some point in your life. When you base your decisions on the truth of who you are, you also remove the obstacle of needing external validation that you are on the right path. You'll get all the validation you need from how it feels on the inside to be on that path.

The process of discovering yourself is beautiful. I discussed this in depth in *Welcome Home*. Discovering who you are involves becoming aware of your habits, patterns, and ways of thinking and being. It urges you to go back to the earliest stories in your life when you began forming beliefs about yourself, your worth, and your place in other people's lives. It requires becoming aware of how you fell into patterns of self-betrayal or abandonment.

If the process of discovering who you are isn't beautiful enough, what comes after is even more beautiful: the part where you radically accept yourself.

How many people get to a point in their lives where they know who they are, but instead of living out their life based on their self-knowledge, they hide the parts they feel ashamed of or that they feel would make them unworthy or excluded? A common example of this is a woman who might realize after she's invested her whole identity in being a mother and caretaker that she wants to invest her time in a passion of hers. She might never reveal that part of her identity out of feeling guilty for wanting to do something for herself. Another more obvious example is with sexual orientation and gender identity. Because these topics are riddled with shame and stigma, so many who don't fit the norm decided by society will hide their true identities out of fear of exclusion. It's possible to spend your life suffering, knowing who you are but not living your truth. It's a lifetime of rejecting and excluding your true self so that others don't reject and exclude you.

When I think back to the period of time when I was exhausting myself during the car-crash period, it became very clear to me that I was someone who was highly sensitive, highly empathetic, a people-pleaser, and a hopeless needer of love.

It pains me to share this. I feel vulnerable admitting to the world how desperate I was for love. I mean, I didn't have a childhood where really "bad" things happened to me. So why can't I just be grateful for that? Over the years, in trying to come to peace with the things I so badly needed, I stopped blaming myself for having those needs and came to understand that what happened to me wasn't in my control and that my feelings at the time were valid.

I used to judge myself for the times in my life when I operated from a place of really needing love. I called myself weak or naive back then. And it's only been the last few years of my life that I look back at those moments with immense self-compassion. I look back at those moments with zero judgment. It's more than nonjudgment; it's also the presence of empathy for myself in a way that I never thought I deserved. I'm grateful that bad things didn't happen to me as a child. I eventually understood that my childhood was hard because of the good things that didn't happen. I needed love. I needed attention. I needed to feel special in moments when any child should feel special. The absence of those moments ingrained in me this belief that the world was indifferent to me. Over the years, I became indifferent to myself as well. When other people around me needed anything, I would work overtime to meet those needs because I knew how it felt to not have those needs met, not ever thinking, *What are my needs and are they being met?*

On your journey to discovering who you are, you will have to confront the moments when you believe you acted out of character. Look back at those moments and remember that you did what you thought was best with the knowledge you had.

Take some time to sit with yourself in those moments and say to yourself exactly that: *What I did was based on the best I thought I could do in the moment.*

You have to give yourself the forgiveness, the understanding, the love, and the safety that you needed in that moment.

During the car-crash period, I began to be more aware of who I was as I wrote. Remember, that was the only authentic thing going on in my life at that time. It took a long time to get from that first glimmer of self-awareness to living my life authentically. First, I had to accept myself. I went through the process of accepting myself for a very long time. During the process, I took some steps to live my life in a way that would honor who I was and give life to a person who was hidden inside of me, the person who my environment taught me wasn't worthy.

For example, I decided to move out of my parent's home at the age of twenty-seven.

I did not feel that I was 100 percent owning that decision at the time. It literally felt like there was no other way for me to continue operating in my life. When I was twenty-six, my writing had taken off, and I was still teaching full-time while completing my full-time doctorate program. In my bustling family home, I was unable to focus on my work. I was very grateful that I had physical safety, that I had a roof over my head, that I didn't have to spend money paying rent or bills, that there was always something for me to eat in the fridge, and that there was a beautiful family with beautiful children around me. But I couldn't do my best work while surrounded by so much noise and chaos. This car-crash period was also an emotional and an identity-crash period. There was no way I could figure out who I was while being so enmeshed in an environment that dictated who I was supposed to be.

This takes me back to the first point I made: being a person of choice allows you to fully own the decisions you make and to keep that in your core as you move forward.

Let me tell you another story. When I moved to Canada from Lebanon at sixteen, what did I do for the next seven years? I lived in a perpetual state of just surviving. Why? Because I was convinced that my life felt as awful as it did because I was made to move from my home country to one that was so different. I felt like I had no choice. I felt out of place partly because I was actually in a new place and partly because it wasn't my choice to be in that place. And I just ended the story there. I blamed my feelings of being out of place on this reality for years. But the truth is, even if reality were different, even if I had gone back to Lebanon, or if I had been the one who decided to move to Canada, I would have felt the same way. Because I still felt out of place in Lebanon and wasn't someone who chose for herself. I was someone who waited for choices to be made for her so she could follow the rules and feel good as a result of being compliant. You can see from this story how early that pattern in my life existed.

There's a difference between doing something in pursuit of the life you want to live and doing something to feel good about yourself. When you do the former, you lead. You choose. You live. When you do the latter, you follow others' rules for what makes you good enough. You are chosen for. And you live someone else's plan for you.

Yes, you could say, *but you were sixteen! What sixteen-year-old has a choice?* I agree with you, but I will also remind you that how that sixteen-year-old operated in the world turned into how that twenty-two-, twenty-four-, twenty-six-, and twenty-eight-year-old operated in the world. I thought that I just had to accept things as they were. And those things often stemmed from other people's choices for me. Or their choices for themselves that included me being a certain way. For example, being a religious person probably would have never been a choice of mine at a younger age. But I lived in a small community, attended an Islamic school, and was surrounded by religion at all times.

Remember, knowing who you are requires taking a holistic look at *your* life. It's not a one-size-fits-all process. Knowing who you are leads to accepting who you are. And once you go through the process of accepting who you are, you can come to the point where you make decisions based on that. You can make a decision about the life you want to live.

3. Tie Your Change to the Life You Want

Let's say the change you are looking to make is to work out more and get into the shape that you desire. What kind of lifestyle would that align with? It would align with the life of someone who invests time in themselves, who keeps promises for themselves, who lives a lifestyle that is fit for them, who sticks to their personal goals, and who has the willpower and determination to effect the changes they want in their life. Do you understand now what I mean by tying your change to the kind of life you want to live?

It doesn't necessarily have to do with a very specific life goal. Remember the moment I described when my grandpa was expressing his love toward my grandma after she died, and how I thought to myself, *that's the kind of love I want?* To say that I want to live a life where the person I'm with is not afraid to express love for me, one where the person I'm with loves me and respects me wholly and wants to build a life with me and include me as part of a team, may sound like a very specific goal, but it really is an overarching life path.

To tie my goal for that kind of relationship with the actions I make in the present moment means that I will reflect on any decision I make that has to do with relationships and ask, *Does this align with the kind of life I know I want to live?* If it doesn't, then I shouldn't move forward with that action.

Let's say you are someone who always falls into a pattern of people-pleasing and you decide that you no longer want to be that kind of person. Let's say you decided that you want to be the kind of person who puts themselves first and isn't influenced by other people's opinions of you. That end goal is beautiful. But what's exponentially more beautiful is the journey you'll take to get to that point. It's the first time you say no to something you don't want to do when you've always said yes. It's the first time you decide that you will not pick up your phone after spending years allowing guilt to decide that you're picking up. It's the first time you make a decision for yourself and your life that disappoints people who had a specific path in mind for you. It's the first time you take that trip you've been wanting to take for so long when you've devoted all your time to being available for everything and everyone else. You get the point. Being on the other side of people-pleasing is beautiful, and it's the journey to get there that makes it beautiful. It's the vulnerability, openness to change, taking risks, putting yourself out there, and trying new things.

Tying your decision to change to the kind of life you want to live will guide you along your journey. And the journey itself, the part where you actually do what it takes to build that kind of life, is what will drive you toward that change. It is that journey that empowers you. It is the journey that brings you closer to who you are because you are, in action, becoming the person who lives the life you want for yourself. And that is not easy. Just as staying in the current situation you're in is not easy, so is the process of getting out of it. Both are hard but only one is familiar. The life you want to live is the unfamiliar one.

For authentic change to occur and be sustained, it's essential to tie it to the kind of life you want to live. You do that by beginning to live as your future self who has already reached the other side. In his book *Atomic Habits: An Easy & Proven Way to Build*

Good Habits & Break Bad Ones, James Clear explains that the best way to build a habit is to tie it to your identity. Do you want to be a writer? What does a writer do? They write every day. So *you* write every day. Instead of aiming to build a habit by focusing on getting to a point where you've built that habit, you should focus on actually practicing it every single day. Similarly, the best way to make and sustain change in your life is to tie it to the life you want to live. And to do what someone living that life would do.

Do you want to live a life of choice? Then choose.

Do you want to live a life with authentic love? Then do what it takes to have that in your life. Maybe you need to end the relationship you're in. Maybe you need to start showing up authentically, vulnerably, and honestly in your relationship. Maybe you need to start loving yourself in the way you want someone to love you. No one knows what you need to do more than you.

Tying your change to a life path maximizes its chances at succeeding. There's a difference between going through with a change because you are intentional with it and going through with a change with no driving purpose. In his book *Drive: The Surprising Truth About What Motivates Us*, Daniel H. Pink reveals that what truly and authentically drives people is actually intrinsic, not extrinsically led by rewards or punishment as we may have thought. In other words, it's not what we are getting from others. Instead, it's what we get from ourselves. According to Pink, intrinsic motivation is made of autonomy, mastery, and purpose. Now you tell me, are those stemming from the outside or the inside? Those all have to do with *you*.

I used to be the kind of person who fixated on my struggle with changes I made instead of focusing on how good the change feels. And that's because I was still driven by external motivation: pleasing my parents, pleasing God, and so on.

When I moved out of my parents' home, I remember constantly feeling like I had done something wrong because, in my culture, a woman only moves out after she gets married. I felt like I was ruining my reputation and my family's. For the longest time, I didn't tell anyone that I moved out. I was afraid to deal with that shame. But the truth was, I was dealing with that shame every day anyway. Perhaps refusing to publicize it wasn't actually about the fear of dealing with it; instead, I didn't share that I had moved out because on some deep level I still believed that what I did was shameful. So for more than a year, I hid that from everyone except my closest friends.

This was an example of a time when I claimed I had no other choice. I felt I had to justify my decision to move out. Like there had to be a reason. And that reason couldn't be that I *chose* to move out, period. So I always said it was because I needed a quiet space to write.

I think back to that now, and I ask myself what would have been so bad about me just wanting to move out and live on my own and experience life the way I wanted? Why was that so shameful? If one of my brothers had made that decision, would it have been as bad? Or as shameful?

The inevitable feelings of exclusion I felt over the next few months were an intense source of pain for me. If you read my "Why can't I have that?" story in *Welcome Home*, you know that from a young age I struggled with feeling like I didn't deserve to be included in love, in belonging, or in being a priority. So doing something that, in my view and that of others, further served my exclusion—or my unworthiness of inclusion—brought about many feelings such as *I deserve this. I brought this exclusion upon myself.*

All I wanted was space for myself. I wasn't choosing to be excluded. I was choosing to do something for myself. I wasn't choosing to disappoint my family or my community. I was choosing myself. And the fact that those two things came at odds with one another (choosing myself and being included) should have been a wake-up call for me. But at the time, it wasn't.

Looking back, I can see the level of control that is involved in coercing someone to believe that they are only worthy of love and belonging when they are a certain way, when they live a certain way, dress a certain way, and when they speak a certain way. I can see that is what kept me chained. Now, I love my own space. I love getting to choose how I dress. I love the fruits of the changes I made.

There has to come a time when you stop dwelling on how hard the change is and its consequences, when you stop dwelling on the unfairness of being put in a position to make a change in the first place and take ownership over your choice. There comes a time when you stop focusing on the losses caused by your change and start feeling how it feels to have that change in your life.

If you continue to judge yourself based on the opinion of those who knew you before you changed, you'll continue to feel like you have been a source of disappointment to them. Remember, you're not choosing to hurt or disappoint them. You are choosing a change for yourself. Their pain and disappointment in you as a result of you not upholding their standards—that's on them to deal with.

It's helpful to keep in mind that your goal is not all the side effects of the change (disappointing others, breaking bonds with others, and so on). Instead, your goal is to make a change in your life that brings you closer to your authentic self and truth.

When guilt pays you a visit, ask yourself honestly and openly, *Am I feeling this guilt because I'm doing something wrong or because I'm breaking a pattern of conditioning that made me believe I only deserve love and belonging without this change?*

4. Bring Your Body in on This Change

We've discussed this before. When you attempt change, though you may be fully on board logically, your body may resist it because it feels like you're going in the opposite direction of the way you normally go.

It's necessary for you to remember that just because you feel your body resisting change, it doesn't mean it's not good for it.

Think of people who have any kind of addiction. They relapse into addiction not because moving on from the addiction isn't good for them, but because moving on from the addiction doesn't feel as good in their body as the addiction did. The addiction is meeting some kind of need, even if the way it does so is by numbing them to reality. It's a shield, a protection, from a reality they fear.

Chapter 1 helped you understand why your body may resist certain changes even though your mind is 100 percent on board. Now you need to keep that in mind as you make change. Among the first things you'll encounter is feeling like you're doing something wrong. Especially if you're a sensitive person, you'll take input from your outer environment that might either deter you from continuing the change or might motivate you to continue living without the change.

If you allow yourself to be ruled by other people's acceptance of you, you'll never move forward in life.

The most important thing, when attempting a change that affects how you are perceived by the people whose opinions you value, is to go inward and feel what it's like to act authentically. At the same time, because you are human and because change isn't so easy, in the moments that you do act in response to external forces, don't immediately go to your mind and judge yourself. Go into your body and feel what it's like to do something that breaks a promise you made for yourself or that goes against what you now want for yourself.

The best example I can give you is when we ask someone

who's in a toxic relationship why they don't leave if "it's so awful." What we don't see is the underlying cycle they're probably going through that looks something like:

Bad behavior directed at you → Wanting to leave → Feeling stuck → Not leaving → Judging yourself for not leaving → Justifying the bad behavior in some way so you don't have to judge yourself for not leaving → The behavior happens again → You judge yourself for not leaving already, and it goes on and on.

If we can interrupt that loop right after the part where the behavior happens and, instead of going to our mind for a judgment or decision, we feel what that behavior elicited in our body, we can become our own seers, hearers, and validators. We become our own shoulders to cry on and our own witnesses.

Consider that you are changing the relationship dynamic with your family. Maybe you became aware that there is a dynamic of enmeshment within your family where everyone's feelings are intertwined, and you feel responsible for the feelings of those around you. This dynamic is characterized by an extreme lack of boundaries and the dismissal of their importance to an individual's healthy development. Enmeshed relationships limit individual expression and personal growth; the needs of one person in the family, or the family as a whole, become paramount over the other individuals' autonomy and desires. Say enmeshment is a dynamic that you decided you no longer want to live by because now you have learned about boundaries. Maybe one of the things you want to change is the level of interaction you have with your family, and they happen to check up on you all the time in a controlling manner. So one of the decisions you make for yourself is that you will limit your availability to them and that you will increase your privacy in your personal life. You've communicated this to them, and you've made it clear that those are your wishes. They respect that for a while, but then it starts happening again; the calls start coming in more intensely, and the attempts at invading your privacy become even more obvious. Maybe you answer the first few calls and don't think anything of it—or you have this feeling in your gut that something isn't right, but you answer anyway. Instead of judging yourself for picking up, go into your body and feel what it feels like every time they call. Become aware. That's what will propel your journey to understand why change has been so hard.

When it comes to dealing with family expectations and obligations as a result of your change, it's important to prioritize yourself. Once you do that, you can stop yourself from being ruled by what they have in mind for you.

Bringing your body in on the change also means you learn more about the trapped traumas in your body and that you actively give them a form of release that liberates you from the hooks those traumas have on you. I will discuss this in depth in the next chapter.

5. Trust Yourself

In the past, every time I would go to a wedding, or worse, an all-girl party, I would dread knowing that I would have to say, "No, I don't dance." The truth was that I didn't know how to dance. And it's not like I ever tried learning. Actually, I never tried dancing, period. I grew up believing that a woman's expression of her femininity or sexuality in any way made her someone who's asking for attention. It made her someone who should be carrying shame. There's a word in Arabic, pronounced *ayb*, that literally means "shame." I would hear it being said to girls and women when it came to raising their voices or wearing something that is considered inappropriate, such as a tight shirt or tight jeans or a short skirt. I would hear it being said if a woman was wearing too much makeup or carried herself in a manner that was seductive in any way. I would also hear it being said to boys and men, but it was more around respect for the elderly or for authority.

Anyway, that should explain why I never danced. When I moved to Canada, I started to be invited to all-girl parties where most of my friends who were there wore the hijab out in public. You might not know this, but a woman who wears the hijab is able to show her hair to other women in private. So I would go to these parties where all my friends would be dressed just like anyone that you would see at any random party. And they would be dancing and having fun. I was very confused because it felt like I was the same person in both settings, private or public. But

I could very clearly see that the women I knew were able to separate the two settings. Maybe I wasn't able to do that because I actually attached shame to femininity, sexuality, having fun, and so on. I obviously didn't attach shame to those things out of nowhere. It was a result of the environment that shaped me to perceive a woman's body and what she chooses to do with it as an invitation for shame.

I am pretty sure when I went to these parties, there was a part of me that judged my friends for being able to just let loose and dance. I don't remember being conscious of that judgment, but looking back, I know that I didn't admire that about them initially and for a while. But after attending a few of these parties and seeing how much fun they had and how good they seemed to feel, I did look at them with admiration and a hint of *I wish I could do that. I wish someone taught me. I wish that I didn't feel so embarrassed to just go up there and dance. Maybe dancing is just not for me.* That's what I convinced myself of.

Fast forward to 2021. I'm thirty-one years old. I'm in my final year of school. We're still in the middle of a pandemic, and the restrictions of face-masking are still in place. I started feeling this itch to begin dance lessons. I was naturally feeling my body move when I heard certain beats. But then something would stop me from fully moving. I didn't know what it was. I went back to the same "maybe dance is just not for me" reason. I remember once going into the bathroom in my empty apartment, putting music on my phone, putting my headphones on, closing the door, turning off the lights, and just dancing. My body felt very disoriented. "Misaligned" is probably a better word. I kept thinking of what I must be looking like dancing this way. I immediately judged myself and stopped. Because I wasn't someone who danced. Can you imagine what *they* would think or say if they saw me dance?! End of the world. Remember this *they* because I'm going to prompt you to identify who that is for you.

I tried dancing in the dark a few times before I just stopped trying altogether. But that itch to dance never went away. So I decided to do something about it. Just like when I wanted to learn how to swim because I never learned when I was younger, I booked private lessons. Even though it was expensive to do that, I decided that if I could spend sixty dollars on a couple of makeup items, I could spend sixty dollars on an hour to learn how to swim. I will tell you about that story at some point, but let's go back to the dancing lessons. I did a simple Google search and found a few dancers in my area and reached out to them. "I just want to learn how to dance if I'm alone or if I'm out at a party and just want to have fun." That's what my email request said. I didn't know what kind of dance genre I would be requesting. I decided to go with a woman named Clara because she seemed to understand that what stopped me from dancing all those years was not limited to just having no experience or knowledge. She understood that it was a much deeper issue that was rooted in shame, fear, ideas of femininity, and trauma.

Our lessons began with simple body movements and stretches. Clara was very quick to point out that I was very flexible and that, physically speaking, certain dance moves are technically not supposed to be hard for me. She wasn't saying that to minimize my fears or underlying shame, but to assure me that while I might be focusing on all the things that were stopping me from dancing, there are many things that will ease my journey to dance. That's the first thing I want you to remember in trusting yourself when you decide to make a change in your life: while you might be held back by all the fears, shame, and any other barriers, know that you already have things about you that will propel you toward that change.

We also did some breathing exercises where I quickly noticed how difficult it was for me to *really* breathe in. In the past, when I would follow different yoga prompts or breathing exercise prompts, I would hear the person saying, "Breathe in. Let it go all the way to your tummy." I would think, *How on Earth would I do that?* My breath always felt like it stopped right at the top of my stomach, and if I didn't release it, I felt like I was going to suffocate.

Looking back, it's clear to me that I was mirroring why I had such a hard time setting boundaries with the people I loved. Every time I would attempt to change my life, I'd feel a hint of that disappointment, shame, and guilt, and instead of fully allowing myself to feel those emotions flow through my body and be released in some way, I would immediately go back on that change because I didn't want to carry that emotion. I was breathing those emotions out before they could really sit in my body out of fear that if I fully held them, I would suffocate. I couldn't handle the feeling of guilt. I couldn't handle the shame. I couldn't handle feeling like I let someone down. Or so I thought. Technically, I could. I could survive, but my body felt like I couldn't.

Remember, your body's survival mode is not the same as what your mind knows. I felt I couldn't survive because my body's survival limits were chained to those relationships that I thought I couldn't survive without. If I fully allowed myself to feel the guilt, shame, and their disappointment in me, I'd be severing the bond I had with those people. And my body just didn't know how to survive without that bond. So my body avoided experiencing the emotions required to sever that bond out of fear of not being able to survive without it.

The sad truth was that by going back on that change or any change I made for myself to avoid the emotions associated with it, I wasn't just going back on that change. I was going back on myself. And I don't say that to judge myself. I say it with self-compassion. It's not like I'm actively choosing to betray or abandon myself. I am choosing what my body associates with survival.

Do you see how pushing myself to do something I'd been wanting to do for so long opened me up to certain parts of my healing? Even if this experience in particular, the dance lessons, didn't push me to make those mind-body connections, it was still an investment in something I really wanted to do for myself. If I knew someone that I loved really wanted to try something, I would gift them that experience without thinking of whether they're going to actually enjoy it or not. So why can't I do that for myself? Why can't you do that for yourself?

It is also essential to ask yourself, *Who comes to mind when I contemplate how others will regard an important change in my life?* Identifying them will lead you to understand much of your conditioning.

This is the next point I want you to highlight: Give yourself opportunities at self-exploration and self-indulgence the way you would give those opportunities to someone you love. Take risks without needing the outcome to be one that's worthwhile based on whatever "worthwhile" meant to you up to now. You get to decide what's worthwhile. You may have been taught that time spent doing things that aren't going to earn money is a waste. You may have been taught that time spent trying new things is risky. You may have been taught that leaving something or someone, like a job or relationship, that is safe and secure for something or someone that is uncertain or unknown is stupid. You may have been taught to fear the uncertain and unknown. Or to stay in something you know will always be there, like a permanent job or a marriage . . . that it is better than risking that security in order to find what makes you happy and feel valued, seen, and heard.

Often what stops us from moving forward with change, whether it's learning how to dance or leaving any kind of relationship that no longer serves our authentic selves, is our fear of what exposing our authentic selves to the world would feel like.

It's one of those things that could chain you for years or even decades, but the moment you fully expose your authentic self, you realize that the only thing you have to lose by not exposing your authentic self is your peace. Anyone who demands you pretend to be someone you're not is someone who does not authentically love you. Maybe they think that their control comes out of love, but you have to remember that authentic love sees you clearly and doesn't aim to chisel you down to a preconceived ideal. Authentic love puts down the chisel and tells you, *I love you as you are. I love you as the old you and the you that you are becoming. I love you as you try new things and as you make decisions for yourself.*

I want you to write down what authentic love for yourself looks like. After you do that, I want you to compare that love to the love you are receiving. This doesn't have to be about romantic relationships—think about all your relationships. It can also be about the love you are giving yourself.

Maybe you're in school, deciding that you want to change the program you're in, and the hardest person on yourself is you. You feel that you're giving up. Or maybe you judge yourself as indecisive. Ask yourself, *Would I speak this way to someone I love? How would I speak to someone I love?* Now speak to yourself that way.

A big part of trusting yourself is giving yourself the grace to not be perfect. You know how Nike goes by "Just do it"? There is a popular TikToker, Elyse Myers, who made a video inviting Nike to put a line after those words so that people could say

"Just do it *scared*," "Just do it *anxious*," "Just do it *uncertain*," and so on. I thought that was one of the most beautiful things I'd ever seen. Once you know a decision is right for you, just move forward with it. Just like when I took the simple step of looking for a dance teacher. Did my fear automatically leave my body when I did that? No. Even the morning before I went to my first lesson, I was driving there thinking, *I hope my car breaks down so that I don't have to go to this. I hope I run out of gas. I hope she's sick and can't make it to this lesson.*

Even after I took steps toward what I knew I wanted to do, I was still subconsciously running away from it because my body was terrified of doing something it associated with shame. But I did it. And once a week, on Tuesday morning, I still had a little bit of that dread, but those lessons pushed me to listen to my body and trust myself in ways that no amount of talking or reading or seeking advice could ever give me. I was showing my body, in action, that I was trusting it. I was showing myself, in action, that I believe in myself. I was showing up for myself. And I was choosing every single week to take a couple of hours to invest in myself.

We don't talk about the little changes that we make every single day, like eating a different meal than the one we ate the day before, taking a different route to work, or chatting with someone new. Those ongoing changes feel normal, and we don't interpret them as saying much about who we are. It'll be easier to own your big changes when you also recognize the smaller changes you make with ease every day. The key point is that you are constantly *making* changes. That is enough evidence that you are capable of *leading* change.

Trust yourself to lead your own path the way you have been trusting other people to lead you your whole life. Why is it so easy for you to trust someone else to get you to the happiness you are seeking, but when it comes to trusting yourself, you think of all the reasons why you're not better at leading yourself than someone else is? Give yourself the grace to not be perfect at your leadership over yourself. To not know the path ahead fully. To take the next step not knowing the outcome for certain. And if you fall, show yourself the compassion you need instead of judging yourself for being a bad leader. You are learning.

CHAPTER 5

Changes We Need to Make

I magine living in a way where you can just be yourself and not have to do anything to be loved as you are. That's what living authentically means. It's not about expecting to be handed love and acceptance for no reason; it's about understanding that the love and acceptance of who you authentically are should never be conditional on hiding or changing parts of yourself. Imagine telling the sun it could only exist if half of its fire was put out. That's what we do to ourselves when we dim our light, when we've been conditioned to believe that our whole light is too much, not possible, or simply wrong.

Here's the story of a woman, let's call her Soul, who grew up in a strict household. Bound by rules to be the best "good girl" she could possibly be, she lived almost thirty years of her life as a compulsive people-pleaser. She did as she was told and was riddled with guilt anytime she even contemplated doing what she wanted for herself. From a young age, she was very aware that to be emotionally safe, she had to cater to her parents' expectations of her. After all, her actions reflected on them. The "better" she was, the more highly regarded they were as "good" parents.

She became a doctor, just like her parents wanted her to. She got every achievement award possible to show her hard work and dedication. When she was younger, her parents enrolled her in extracurriculars, including an art class where she started creating unique abstract pieces of art. She carried that into her adult years and often donated pieces to charities—something which made her parents very proud.

One day, she got an email from a man named Matt saying he'd won one of her donated pieces at a fund-raising dinner and was wondering if he could order ten more canvases for his business offices. Soul was surprised but also happy. She took photos of all the pieces she had and uploaded them for his view. He picked the ones he liked and paid her two hundred dollars per piece.

A couple of weeks later, she got another email inquiring about her prices. And then another. These were from some of Matt's employees and their clients. She sent them the same online gallery she'd shown Matt and sold a couple more pieces. One night, at dinner with her family, she brought up this exciting string of events. "Someone reached out to me a couple weeks ago after winning one of my pieces at that hospital fund-raising dinner from last year. And I've sold more than ten pieces since then!" No one said a word. There was just silence. Feeling shame spreading through her body, she said, "Isn't that exciting?!"

Her dad responded, "You're a doctor, and this is what you're excited about?"

Pause here and reflect on any personal experiences like this, not just with family. Sit with the feeling a situation such as this elicits in your body. How would you describe it?

This was a defining moment for Soul. She felt that something she really cared about was yet again belittled and not celebrated. And even though she had endured that throughout her thirty years of life, this time was different. Something in her changed. She experienced *that* moment.

You know the moment I'm talking about. In almost every movie, show, book, or real-life story, there's always that one moment when the main character makes a life-changing realization that gives them so much clarity. It's the moment when the music turns from sad to uplifting, and the person starts making every change that they've been needing to make to be their true authentic selves.

This is what Soul did. She decided that if her art meant something to *her*, that was enough to continue focusing on it. And she did. She faced a lot of criticism from her family, but the joy she felt finally doing what she loved was much bigger than the pain she felt because of her parents' disappointment. With time, Soul opened her own art gallery and school. She never got the "I'm proud of you" she knew, deep down, she wanted from her parents. And she made peace with that. As time went on, and she fully transitioned from being a full-time doctor to a full-time art school owner, she took her life back into her hands and paved her own road. Nothing is more liberating than that.

Have you had your moment yet? If yes, reflect on how it felt. If not, reflect on moments that could've been that moment for you. Maybe you have an inkling that you haven't been living fully authentically; sometimes we hide this knowledge from ourselves. As you read the next few sections outlining ways to move toward an authentic life, you will get signs and signals that will reveal to you how you've been living inauthentically. Be open to receiving those; take some time to sit with them, even journal about them. These are the markers guiding you to your true happiness.

1. Stop Trying

What if I just stopped trying? What if I just stopped caring altogether? What if I just no longer cared about what people thought?

I remember the sensation in my body when these words crossed my mind. It was a true moment of alignment and harmony between my mind and body. I was done—done carrying the weight of other people's opinions, done feeling like I was in the spotlight of a few people around me. I was done trying to control how others saw me and done trying to make sure they always saw me as good and perfect.

Previously, any time I would try to change my life in a way that felt more like the real me, I would immediately reverse course. It would be followed by weeks, sometimes even months, of feeling down and sad in a hopeless and desperate kind of way. I was waiting for the people around me to approve the changes I wanted to make, fully knowing I was never going to get that approval. So instead of taking that as a sign to stop seeking their approval, I would try to negotiate with them how important that goal, the goal of becoming more myself, was. To live the life that I knew I wanted to live, I would have to prioritize my authenticity above all else.

I went through a really long period when I would go to one specific coffee shop attached to a bookstore. I would take my journal with me and sit there for hours. I would write what I was experiencing in the moment and see where it would lead me. Not surprisingly, it always led me to my childhood and my need not only for love but my desperate need to feel seen, heard, and valued . . . to feel like I was someone. This was more than ten years ago, before I discovered inner child healing was even a thing and before I discovered it was a form of therapy that helps restore your sense of autonomy and self-worth by guiding you in reconnecting with the part of you that experienced trauma, pain, or abandonment as a child. Connecting with your inner child helps you understand how your early experiences in life shaped you to be who you are today. It also allows you to step in as your current adult self to guide your inner child in making sense of past events that you were helpless in navigating at the time, which resuscitates your self-trust and allows you to live a more conscious life.

For my whole life, I had felt like I lived in the shadows of the woman I was supposed to be. I can't remember any moments when I experienced true internal peace. Any peace I felt was just the absence of turmoil, but never authentic peace. Living in this shadow meant that I didn't truly perceive myself as a separate entity from my family, religion, and culture. Basically, I viewed myself as an extension of those three and, without them, I felt that I wasn't attached to anything. Being expelled by them spelled out danger to me because being attached was one of my fundamental needs as a human.

Newsflash! Being attached is one of every human's fundamental needs. In his book *The Myth of Normal: Trauma, Illness & Healing in a Toxic Culture*, Dr. Gabor Maté discusses how every human has two fundamental needs: attachment and authenticity. *Attachment* spells out the need to be connected to an entity, to feel cared for, seen, and heard. *Authenticity* stands for being who you are and not attaching your worth to what you do. The tragedy is when your attachment is threatened by your authenticity. Basically, behaving authentically can threaten the attachments you have to people you think you need. That is truly what I went through. My welcome was dependent on following a rule book written by family, culture, and religion. When I didn't follow those rules, I immediately felt like something was off, like something was wrong. And I took that to mean that something was wrong *with me*. That should have been my wake-up call.

Feeling excluded didn't mean that I did something to deserve that exclusion. Or that I *was* someone who fundamentally deserved that exclusion. If my inclusion was dependent on my not doing something that is right for me, then that wasn't authentic inclusion. It was conditional inclusion. And the word "conditional" goes against everything that "inclusion" stands for. I just didn't want that anymore.

So I decided to just stop trying. I decided to just let myself be and let the world fall apart around me if it had to. Maybe that's what needed to happen. At least my world wouldn't be falling apart as a result of trying to keep the world around me intact. And let me tell you, you learn a lot about your place in people's lives when you stop trying to please them or get their approval. People tried guilting me into regressing to the girl who cared about everyone's feelings. "You changed," "What's up with you?" and "I can't believe you said/did that!" became normal things for me to hear. I was given the cold shoulder and silent treatment. I was even flat-out told, "If you don't go back to the way you were before [that is, to being the nice, good girl who dressed 'modestly' and cared about what people say and think], you're no longer in my life." The good news is, I didn't let that stop me. I realized that those who don't respect my growth, my change, don't have *my* best interests in mind.

Here's an affirmation that will help you on this journey: My energy will go toward making the change(s) I need to live more authentically. How the world around me reacts is theirs to handle.

2. Don't Negotiate Your Change with Those Who Want You to Stay the Same

On your journey to your most authentic life, your story will reveal itself. It will narrate itself in different tones, carrying different messages, and all you have to do is listen and understand. Without judgment. Without the need to rewrite it. Give it only radical acceptance.

Writing this chapter ripped me apart as I realized how hard I've fought on this journey. It's one thing to talk about living authentically and another to live authentically, as I learned. It's very hard to take action, because that's where the consequences lie.

As I thought about living my most authentic life, the first emotion that bubbled up in my body was anger. Weird, right? Why would I feel angry? Because it dawned on me how every time in my life when I made a decision for myself, I had to battle so much negativity around me. It had gotten to the point where I couldn't even enjoy the changes I made. It felt like I was running an obstacle course filled with potholes to avoid. So the relief I felt after I was done making the change wasn't about the change itself, but about my ability to achieve some damage control. I was just so relieved that I was still tolerated by my community (that's before I learned that tolerance and acceptance are not the same thing).

Who wants that?

No one. But that's what I accepted.

I want to share with you the airplane story. I often come back to this story because there's so much to unpack. When I decided to take my hijab off, I started putting out feelers in front of my family. The first time I mentioned that I was thinking about it, my dad was upset. He very abruptly said, "Don't even think about it!"

When I first heard my dad say that, I immediately fell into shame. Like how could I have even contemplated doing something that is so forbidden? But then I did the complete opposite of what he told me to do. I continued to think about it. And by continuing to explore that thought, I grew so much. I started questioning everything in my life. In retrospect, it was necessary for me to push the limits of how far I had control over my life. Instead of the governing body over my decisions being the triumvirate of family, religion, and culture, it had to be . . . me. I no longer wanted to be controlled. I wanted to control my own life. Not just control, but lead.

I continued to bring the topic up every once in a while, in the form of negotiating, trying to explain why it was okay for me to take my hijab off. But the response I always got was, "You shouldn't do this. You're being influenced badly."

Eventually, I stopped bringing the topic up but also stopped visiting my family as often as I did before. One day, my mom called and said my dad wanted to talk to me. I hesitated at first. *Why does he want to talk to me? To tell me again why I was making the wrong decision?* My mom assured me it was going to be a good conversation. I told her that I reserved the right to get up and leave if I felt uncomfortable. She said that was okay.

I arrived at their house. I was shaking. It was my *dad*. The man who I wanted to please my whole life. And I'm the youngest in the family, so we had a special bond. We sat at opposite ends of the same couch. He looked at me and said, "I've been thinking about this whole thing, and I understood that the reason I was so resistant to accepting your decision is that I was worried about you. I was worried that you were having an identity crisis. You're just at the beginning of your writing career, and I didn't want you to come across as shaky or not sure about who you are. Like, you know when an airplane is taking off, it's very important that it's steady and very well-aligned. Any little mistake or shakiness has the potential to make it go down. But then I thought about it even more. You're not just taking off. You're already up in the sky among the stars. You're steady and confident in who you are. So, I shouldn't worry about you."

First, a metaphorical jaw dropped. And then I cried. I did not expect my dad to say this. This was one of the very few positive reinforcements that I got from him in my entire life. And it took months of me sticking to my decision and moving toward my autonomy. In that moment, I was so relieved that my dad finally came around. But now when I look back at that moment, I hate that such a moment was one of the few positive connections I experienced with my dad throughout my entire life.

The moral of the story is, it doesn't matter if you're just taking off or if you're shaky as you move toward the life you know is right for you. Do not negotiate the validity of your change with anyone. You can discuss it with them, go over the pros and cons, the possible obstacles, and so on, but do not negotiate to get permission. You are the leader of your life.

In the process of forgiving myself for expending so much of my energy on getting the approval of my parents and others, I realized that out of the forgiveness needed to come a promise to myself moving forward. Never again will I negotiate my choices for myself with anyone. Never again will I consider the approval of others to be a necessary ingredient in my change toward an authentic life for me.

3. Live Outside of Survival Mode

In talking to my therapist about setting boundaries with members of my family, I explained how I would immediately feel flooded with guilt because I felt I owed my family a certain level of allegiance. And even though that allegiance breached my privacy and my life choices, I still felt like it was my responsibility to figure out a way to make my life one that wouldn't put my relationship with them in jeopardy. The notion that family and reputation is more important than anything else was so ingrained in me. What I realized after extensive therapy and introspection is that I was trying hard to keep the bond I had with my family at any expense, even though the relationship I had with them was dependent on me living my life in a way they approved. What that meant was that anytime I did something I knew they wouldn't approve of, they were sitting somewhere in the back of my head telling me that I was bad. Say that I wore a dress that was a little too short or a little too "revealing;" I would hear their voices in my head telling me I shouldn't be dressed that way. And the worst part is that, in the front-row seat, no one other than myself was claiming, *you are doing something wrong*. I became an echoing critic; echoing their voices about me to me.

So, here's a life rule for you: Don't be an echoing critic of yourself. Be an advocate for yourself instead.

Even after I ventured into living my life in a way that felt authentic to me, I was still allowing the bond with my family to tell a story about myself that wasn't true. That bond was telling me that my authenticity was simply a phase of rebellion, a period of my life that I would eventually regret. That bond was telling me that my true intentions weren't to live my life authentically, but to hurt my family. That bond was telling me that I had to keep my authenticity secret because if I exposed it, that bond would be severed. It felt like I had been living my whole life on a ship that had a hole at the bottom. It was my responsibility to keep my foot on that hole to prevent the ship from sinking. Naturally that meant I couldn't venture very far. It also meant that even when I tried to venture far, I always feared the possibility that the ship would sink or that a disaster would happen. It was 100 percent my responsibility to keep the ship afloat. That ship was floating on an ocean of my authenticity, and the hole was the only way for my authenticity to come through. I still allowed a tiny bit of my authenticity through but not enough to sink the ship.

This was my survival mode.

How sad is it to think that the price of my authenticity was connection with the people I loved the most? With the people I still love the most. With the people who I know loved me and still love me. I know I love them without condition. I know that I never gave myself permission to question or judge or get into any aspects of their lives. I know that it doesn't matter what they choose for themselves, I would still love them because I love them for who they are, not for what they do or for what they choose for themselves. And that's all I ever wanted in return; to be unconditionally loved.

Perhaps the biggest indication for me of both those truths, the fact that I love them without condition and the fact that I just want them to love me without condition, is that I couldn't write this whole part without crying.

I don't blame them for being the way they are. Even though I do have moments of anger, I don't blame them. I empathize with them because that's how they were raised. That's what they were taught. That's what they tied their goodness and worth to. That's what they truly believe it means to be a good dad, a good mom, a good brother, and a good sister. They see it as being protective of me. They see it as making sure that no one has one bad word to say about me. They see it as being a good example for me because they've seen more of the world than I have. What I wished they would see is their protection caused a lot of emotional unavailability on their part, which shaped a belief within me that my emotions were a burden that had no place to go.

Anyone who knows me personally knows how hard it is for me to ask anyone for help. I started working when I was sixteen years old. I paid my way through university by working and taking student loans. There were a couple of times when I borrowed money from my brothers, who were always there for me that way, but I did it only because the loans I was getting were going to be late, and I didn't want to be charged any late fees. I would promise my brothers that I would pay them back in a couple of days as soon as the money came in. Still, I felt like such a burden doing so, not because they made me feel that way but because I learned to be independent. Because I never wanted anyone to think that I depended on them for anything.

A few months ago, I was having a rough week with my mental health, directly related to this war of authenticity versus attachment I was experiencing. I hadn't gone shopping and had run out of food in my fridge. Lying in bed, feeling very weak and alone, I called my sister and asked if she could get me some groceries. She didn't ask any questions. She just said, "I'll be there soon." She came over to my place with a cart of groceries that could feed a family even though I lived alone. She proceeded to put the groceries away while I sat on the couch visibly recovering from a few days of crying. She made tea. And then sat next to me.

"What's going on?" she asked.

I told her how I'd been struggling with feeling lonely. And she immediately said, "Well, why haven't you been coming over?"

I knew she would say something like that, so I told her that even when I come over, I still feel lonely because I feel like I can't fully be myself. I must be filtered and guarded to feel like I'm accepted or welcomed by everyone in the family.

I told her that when anyone reaches out to me, it seems that their biggest concern is where I am and who I'm spending my time with. They throw guilt and shame on me for not coming to visit instead of asking how I'm doing or showing genuine concern for my happiness or well-being.

She immediately said, "Of course, we care about you and how you're doing. We just want to make sure that you're not doing anything that would hurt you."

I replied, "I just want to feel like you see all the good things I'm doing in the world. I help so many people put words to their thoughts and emotions. I've been in school for as long as I can remember, and I'm almost done with my doctorate program. I spend so much of my time doing work to continue to be independent and self-sustaining. And I don't ever feel celebrated by any of you. I just feel like that's the bare minimum I could do to just be perceived as okay by all of you."

So, my sister said, "You know, at the end of the day, you're my sister. It doesn't matter what you do or how you live your life, you'll always be my sister and I accept you."

At this point, I felt this tug of sadness in my heart. I said,

"But I don't just want to be accepted, as in you tolerate me and my authentic life. I want to feel like there isn't an undertone of *but I wish you were different*."

That was a really good conversation we had. I was proud of myself for being able to open up in that way instead of continuing to internalize how unseen I felt with them.

I also felt like this conversation made a difference for my sister. Because since then, she calls to see how I'm doing. She doesn't ask me where I am or what I'm doing or pressure me to come over and visit. She enthusiastically congratulates me anytime I share a new accomplishment with her. And she respects when I tell her that there are certain things I don't want to talk about when she asks me.

I did what I had to do. I communicated what I was feeling and asked for what I needed in our relationship. You should do the same with the people in your life. And if they fail to give you what you need, you must decide how important that bond is.

In that same conversation, my sister also helped me recognize my sensitivity. Because she saw that I was in a state of on-and-off crying.

She said, "You're very sensitive."

I responded, "Yes. I am. And that's no longer something that I will apologize for to anyone. I embrace that as part of who I authentically am."

She said to me, "Yes. I think that's what differentiates you from so many people out there. It's why you're able to write as beautifully as you do. It's why you're able to help so many people put words to their feelings. I can't do that. None of us can. That's your gift. But this is where I think you need to make a change. I think you have to turn off your sensitivity in your day-to-day life outside of your writing. Because to be constantly emotionally invested in and affected by anything that happens around you will just drain you."

Indeed, I had a very hard time drawing a line between what was going on around me and my internal emotions. It's not something I'm ashamed of. I think it's what allows me to truly understand what people go through. But she was right.

When I reflected on this moment of connection with my sister, I understood that she was trying to protect me from being so emotionally invested in the well-being of everyone around me. And I had to remind her that I needed her to stop trying to protect me and to instead embrace with me what makes me authentically me.

Back to the ship analogy. To live your authentic life, you must decide, which ship do you want to be on? The survival mode one or the authentic mode one? Which compass do you want to use to direct you? The conditions others put to you or your choices for yourself? What do you want your north to be? Your authentic life, where, yes, you might not be in the lives of those whom you so badly want to please, where you might not be considered a good person by some, but you are living your truth? Or a life of pleasing others?

Breaking the bonds that feel as though they're holding you captive is difficult. And more than being difficult, it's freeing.

Freedom will be scary. It will be scary to sink the survival mode ship.

It'll feel scary and lonely for a while, but once you learn that it is impossible to drown in your own authenticity, you will learn to swim in it and you'll see how essential it is to your well-being. You'll be at peace with the fact that breaking any bond outside of you is okay if it means mending the bond you have with yourself.

4. Break the Bonds That Hold You to an Inauthentic You

This section will be about trauma bonds as they are, in my view, the hardest bonds to break. But to live an authentic life, breaking those bonds is paramount. Dr. Nicole Lepera, a holistic psychologist, defines *trauma bonds* as "relationships where there are cycles of emotional neglect, abuse, abandonment, violation of boundaries, controlling dynamics, enabling, shaming, push/pull, or punishment dynamics." These dynamics begin with our parents or caregivers and when we don't heal them, we reenact and relive them in our romantic relationships. Through our romantic partners, we try to correct our experiences of familial neglect, abandonment, emotional and physical abuse, and so on. This is incredibly addictive, even when we know it's bad for us. One thing you must remember about a bond is that it requires two people. You're not the only participant in this. The two of you feed off each other in some way and subconsciously reenact patterns. Whether this trauma bond is with a parent, romantic partner, friend, or even coworker (yes, it happens!), breaking it is difficult.

It's like a drug you know is bad for you, but you feel like you can't live without it. When it comes to people, imagine you're in a relationship with someone who often puts you down with demeaning words and behaviors. They treat you like you mean absolutely nothing to them. Then one day, out of the blue, without you expecting it, they show you kindness. Because moments like that are so rare, they mean a lot to you. It's only after you have a healthy distance from them that you realize there was nothing great about those moments other than the fact that they were so rare, and you felt special because someone who rarely shows you kindness is showing it to you. Those moments that were given to you so easily at first, then turned into a rarity, are a reminder of the times when they were your normal. And the bond gets stronger.

Are you bound by any trauma bonds? Take a minute to reflect on this.

When this happens with parents, it's often harder to come to terms with it because our parents are usually present in our lives since before we can remember. They set the dynamic of what's normal and what's not, what's right and wrong. To a certain extent, we perceive them as perfect, so if they do or say something, we take it as law. As we grow, we realize that they are not perfect, that they too have healing to do, and that they were bound by certain rules, like we are.

You have to work on breaking the bonds that hold you to an inauthentic life. The first step is becoming aware of them. Then you can work on breaking them. And remember, breaking bonds with past versions of yourself requires breaking bonds with those who conditioned you in the past to be a certain way. That doesn't necessarily mean breaking the whole relationship, but it does mean building a healthy, boundary-full relationship in which you don't have to sacrifice your authenticity for that bond to persist.

As I mentioned previously, I experienced resentment toward myself when I started breaking bonds. But then I experienced resentment toward my family. "How could *I* let myself down?" turned into "How could *they* let me down?" In that resentment, I assumed that they intended to make me feel unworthy of love and affection. I knew and still know that they are good people. They'd never willingly do something like that, but I'd always wonder, *How could you not have known that leaving me behind for so long, and that not connecting with me emotionally, was wrong?*

Maybe that resentment served a purpose. It allowed me to validate my experience, voice healthy anger, and move into an authentic life that was free of that resentment. This is part of breaking trauma bonds: validating your experience, allowing your anger to be released, and no longer trying to change the relationship dynamic. You instead see it for what it is, accept it, and decide whether you want to continue being part of it or not. If you decide you want to continue with them, then you have to create boundaries.

It helps to evaluate why you so badly want to keep a bond with someone who only loves you, welcomes you, and sees you as worthy when you are not yourself. I know that's a big ask, so let's break it down. One thing I struggled with when I was trying to live authentically was wanting others to think like me. If my reasoning was logical, they should be convinced once I explain it, right? During my master's in education program, a professor told us in our very first class, in an effort to get us to think outside the box, that common sense is not always *good* sense. That stuck with me. Take a minute to think about those words and what they mean to you in your current situation. Your common sense is based on how you were raised, your environment, community, and so on.

Common sense is not always general sense. It's not always what makes sense to everyone. It's not always ethical sense. It's not always fair sense. It's not always peaceful, respectful, loving sense. Give yourself permission to question what is considered "common sense," and don't try so hard to fit within the limits of what's common sense to others. Your story and who you are don't have to fit anywhere that makes no room for them.

Letting go of the life that you thought was the most you could ever achieve is messy and uncomfortable. It requires you to face the consequences of not following the path you didn't draw out for yourself in the first place. Many of us are willing to never go after the life we want because what feels like a journey of rebellion is not worth the connections lost. Now that you've read it, it feels like a punch in the gut, right? Why would you want a "connection" with someone who is not connecting to *you*, but to the filtered, unwhole, hiding you. That's not a wholesome connection. It's a conditional one. And you have to start taking inventory of all the connections in your life and determine whether they're authentic based on you being authentic or whether they are constant reminders for you to work hard to prove you're worthy.

5. Let Your World Revolve Around *You*

Let your world revolve around you so that you are the leader. Let your world revolve around you, because if it doesn't, it will revolve around others. You don't want that. You want to make sure you operate in this world from a place of choice. From a place of knowing that the only thing within your direct control is you and your behavior. If you don't let your world revolve around you, you will revolve around your world. You won't be an active participant in your life, but a responder, a reactor.

Let your world revolve around you by giving yourself permission to change your life and all that's within it. Let your world revolve around you by asking yourself what you really want for yourself. Reflect on why you're living your life the way you are and according to whom. When seeking your authentic truth, don't limit yourself to how far you were taught you should go. Don't aim for living your authentic life in the shadows. In the short term, sometimes making changes in secret serves your protection. And that's okay. But in the long run, you don't want to always be hiding. You need to work at distancing yourself from the places that do not welcome your authentic self. Don't try to pretend you're someone you're not just to avoid being excluded or ostracized. Put your need to be who you authentically are above your need to be included or accepted.

Let your world revolve around you by no longer seeking permission from those you spent so much of your time, heart, and soul seeking approval. Have you ever considered that their permission may not be what is best for you? I mean, they're human just like you are. They can't be perfect, just like you can't be perfect. They went through life in a way that is different from your life. So why is their acceptance so important that you are willing to do whatever it takes to please them? I know that sounds harsh. And it sounds like I'm being judgmental. But all I'm saying is, I understand. I get it. It's hard to break away from the storyline we were always fed. It's hard to go against the grain. It's hard to be the one who stands out in a way that is considered negative. It's hard to break out of your conditioning.

I have a friend who recently shared a story on her Instagram account about a book she had read on boundaries. She spoke about how it inspired her to cut off contact with her father and how hard that was for her to do. She talked about the feeling of guilt that took over her for the next few weeks because, at the end of the day, it was her dad. She felt like she was being a bad daughter and a bad human. But she decided that the healthiest thing for her to do was to no longer give access to someone who was trying so hard to control her in her thirties. Remember when we talked about the pain of realizing that the survival mode ship is finally sinking? And how it takes a while to learn to swim in your authenticity? The weeks my friend was experiencing guilt, shame, and the overall feeling she was doing something wrong represent that awkward transition phase.

This leads me to my next point.

Let your world revolve around you by not constantly feeling like you're doing something wrong. Own it. Don't close your eyes when the explosion of your authentic life happens. Open your eyes to the glory unfolding in front of you.

In order to live your life authentically, you have to be willing to tell your story just as it is. No sugarcoating. No excusing. No minimizing. No trying to protect those who caused you pain. None of that. This is not about telling your story publicly for the world to see or access. If that's what you want, go ahead. But telling your story publicly is not a necessary part of owning your story. Telling your story to yourself exactly as it is, validating every part of it for yourself, as ugly as it may be, is a necessary part of owning your story. Don't change certain details based on what you believe about the intentions of those who hurt you. Write the story from your perspective. Write how it made you feel. This is not about them. It's not about making them look bad. If what they did happened to be bad, then the bad part isn't that you chose to talk about it. The bad part is what they did.

Sometimes what stops us from admitting to ourselves that others hurt us as badly as they did is because we know, deep down, what we need to do next. It could be starting to build a boundary with them, which may lead to a more distant relationship or none. It could be immediately cutting them off. It could be confronting them about it. But we subconsciously avoid truly and clearly allowing ourselves to see the truth of what happened to shelter ourselves from the pain that will come from us getting tired of carrying that truth so clearly.

When the truth becomes heavy, but you continue carrying it out of fear that letting it fall will break something, maybe you need to let it fall. Maybe that truth is demanding to be dropped so it can break the reality that's beneath you. And when you let it fall, you will feel light enough to leap to a different reality.

A question that might still be looming over you is: How on Earth do I live an authentic life? Even when you don't know how to live authentically, you know very well when you're not. You know! Trust yourself. Living authentically will never feel like something from which your body truly wants to escape. It might feel like you want to escape because those around you don't approve, but never because you don't feel true alignment and peace.

Look at the way you're living and ask yourself, *Is it authentic to me? Or is it authentic to the way I've been conditioned to live, speak, act, and be?*

Only you know the ways in which you're living inauthentically.

Trust yourself.

Only you know what is genuinely authentic to you.

Trust yourself.

Only you can decide to make changes in order to live that most authentic life.

Trust yourself to lead yourself.

CHAPTER 6

When Change Doesn't Go as Expected

U nless you're too young to remember, you've probably heard about Brad Pitt and Jennifer Aniston's split in 2005. During one of her interviews with Oprah, Jennifer was addressing her recovery from their breakup. She told Oprah that she was with a friend after one of their yoga sessions, and she experienced a feeling that she didn't believe she'd ever experienced before. "I don't want to be anywhere other than where I am right now," she said and went on to explain that she was not sitting somewhere dwelling on the past, that she was not fretting or obsessing about something in the future. It was just a feeling of total peace.

When Oprah asked how she got there, Jennifer said that you can read all the self-help books and understand them logically, but you'll get stuck in figuring out the *how* of it all. You might get sad because you're not there yet. Then you just realize one day that it happened. She referred to the yoga session with her friend as that moment for her.

What's your moment? Has it happened yet? Reflect on that.

If you haven't experienced this moment yet, you might be waiting for the magical feeling when you see and feel deep into your soul in a crystal clear way that you've healed. That you've accomplished the ending of this change. That you got to the other side. You may want some kind of indication that you're there. It helps to remember that life is messy, uncertain, and unpredictable. Your life is not a game you play on your phone where you get a message indicating when you've completed a level, or the whole game. Your life is not a show or movie where you get the powerful, celebratory inspirational music playing in the background when you've accomplished your change. Your life is real. Whether it's right after a yoga class with your friend or in front of the whole class, right after you finished buying your groceries or as you're making a meal, or a random moment at work or right before you go to sleep, you will know when that moment comes. It will feel like total peace. And you might choose to celebrate it by yourself or with someone who really cares about you, but either way, nothing will take away from the power of that moment.

Sometimes the toxicity from a certain experience you went through takes time to cleanse out of your mind, body, and soul. And there's no telling how long that will take. But you will know when it has happened. I know it sounds clichéd, but it happens when you are least looking for it. I often wondered why that is, and here's what I've learned. Sometimes it is not what we went through or how bad it was or the fact that we didn't get closure that holds us back, but our attachment to it all. Our attachment to wanting it to be different. Our attachment to wanting to know why it happened. Our attachment to wanting to get past it. Attachment to anything outside of us detaches us from ourselves. Above all, what you need to believe is that you, outside of everything that happened to you, are okay. You are enough. You need to be able to spend time and distance away from it all to be able to get to a reality where the change that happened is not central to your life. That is how you prove to yourself, in action, that you can survive and thrive past it.

One of the most powerful ingredients on your journey through change is acceptance. Acceptance of the messiness, the imperfection, and the vulnerability that seems to flood you as you try to get to the other side. There will be days when you will feel frustrated and say, "Isn't it about time this is over? When will I stop hurting?" You're indirectly judging yourself for feeling pain, a normal human experience. Your ability to acknowledge the pain of a hurt that was thrown at you is part of what makes you who you are. Thank the part of you that feels the pain of injustice, dishonesty, disrespect, unfairness, [insert the pain you are going through right now]. Thank that part for protecting you from perceiving what's wrong as okay. Having the ability to feel the pain is a gift. Don't judge yourself for having it. Truly, no one wanted to believe more than I did that making myself a cold-hearted person would fix all my problems. It just doesn't work that way. Closing yourself off to feeling pain closes you off from feeling happiness and joy too. It also keeps you living right on the surface of life. Going deep will be something to avoid at all costs. Because you can't go deep without getting past the pain that's waiting to be felt by you. While it might be a healthy stage of your healing, it's not healthy to stay there. Staying there will make you unable to connect with others. More sadly, it will make you unable to connect with yourself. So while you may hate how painful growing is, try to acknowledge how uncomfortable it is to be going through it. Try to sit compassionately with yourself through it instead of judging yourself. Before you say, "But isn't it about time I'm there?!" remember that the bigger the change, the longer it will take for you to get there. Not only are you making choices for yourself, but you are also dealing with the changes that happen as a result of your choices.

1. Be Realistic with the Timing of Your Change

One of my all-time favorite movies is *P.S. I Love You*. I was seventeen years old when it came out. That would've been my second year of living in Canada, during my first year of university. It was before I got into reading books in English. When the movie came out, I didn't even know it was based on a book.

The whole movie is about Holly grieving the death of her husband, Gerry, who had a brain tumor. He has written a series of letters to her that start arriving shortly after his death, each one ending in the words, "P.S. I love you."

There's one scene close to the end of the movie, after the main character, Holly, takes a trip with her friends to Ireland, where she and her late husband first met, when her friends Sharon and Denise share their news that one of them is getting married and the other is having a baby. It was obvious how uncomfortable this news made Holly. But they don't tell us why yet.

A couple scenes after this, Holly visits Gerry's parents, where they give her a letter that Gerry had left for her. In this letter, he recalls meeting her for the first time on a random road. He walks with her to guide her back to her hotel. In the letter, he tells her how he fell in love with her wild spirit and her open and free outlook on the world. He writes, "I don't worry about you remembering me. . . . It's that girl on the road you keep forgetting. 'My business is to create. It doesn't even matter what you do.' You told me that, remember? P.S. So go home. Go find it. Find that thing that makes you like nobody else. I'll help. Look for a sign."

Right after this scene, the movie cuts to a montage with music in the background showing Holly returning to her home in the United States. We then hear multiple answering machine tones, with voice messages left by her friends and her mom, with obvious irritation from their end that she hasn't been answering their calls or communicating with them. During this time, you see Holly brainstorming possible careers she could pursue, writing pro and con lists and business goals of how much money she wants to make. It's clear that she's getting nowhere. Then "3 weeks later" comes up on the screen.

Holly is now sitting on her couch watching television, and the shoes on the actress catch her attention. Then, her phone rings, and it's her friend Denise telling her that she's not invited to her wedding anymore. So Holly throws the remote at her answering machine, which topples over a picture of her and Gerry. She gets up to fix it and comes across one of Gerry's broken suspender clasps that she had placed randomly on a shoe.

Again, the movie cuts to another montage, showing Holly drawing out shoe designs and taking a shoemaking class. "Autumn" comes up on the screen. And it's clear from the change in weather and attire that it's months later. Holly has finally discovered "the thing that makes her like nobody else" and starts designing shoes.

The whole movie is two hours long. The scene in which Gerry tells Holly to go find the thing that makes her like nobody else comes after the hour-and-a-half mark. Almost the whole movie is showing her grief and struggle with letting her husband go. Guess how much time lapses between Gerry telling her to go find the thing and her finding it? The thing that represents the rediscovery of passion and the creation of an authentic life?

Four minutes. All of that happened in mere minutes.

And that's why we love watching movies and shows. They often show the beauty of having revelations, epiphanies—and then they show the wonderful results of those breakthroughs. But for the most part, that in-between part is usually a few scenes with music in the background, a few words here and there. It's sped up. The scenes slow down after the full change has happened. Wouldn't it be incredible if that's how things worked in real life? Imagine what it would be like if we could gloss over when the transition is happening. A change that is quick and beautiful seems glamorous and exciting. The reality is that transitions are typically difficult and uncomfortable.

What took four minutes in that movie would have taken at least a few months in real life. It's hard enough to come to realize that you need to make a change in your life, let alone making the decision. The hardest part after deciding is the execution part. It's the planning, the gauging of how realistic the goal is, and how much time it requires. It's writing down all the supports you will need along the way, whether those supports are human, financial, or even motivational. The minute-to-minute part of getting through every day realistically once you've decided to pursue a certain change can be as hard as it can be exciting. There will be ups and downs, moments when you feel like you've accomplished so much in moving toward the reality that you're working for, and moments when you feel like you've taken ten steps back. You might even sometimes regret deciding to make this change and question whether it was right for you.

Most of us want the guarantee that if we go for a change, it will be worth it. Whether making a career change, beginning a new relationship, or moving to a new country, we want a guarantee that our choice will be worthwhile. More than that, we want the journey from our current reality to our desired or authentic reality to be one that is full of excitement and ease. If, instead, the journey is difficult and frustrating, we take it as an indication that maybe this change isn't the right one.

When the change you embark upon doesn't go as you expected, reflect on what your expectations were to begin with. If you expected excitement and ease, the absence of those two will cause disappointment. If you expected excitement and ease interspersed with moments of hardship, unfamiliarity, fear, uncertainty, exhaustion, loneliness, and even moments of needing to sit down and evaluate where you are and what you need to do next, then when those things happen you won't be disappointed. Instead, you will feel like it is all a normal part of change.

You might hear people who talk about manifestation say that expecting the worst to happen will invite it to happen. Or that even contemplating the possibility of something bad or negative happening will bring it to you. The intention is to keep you from being focused on the negativity that could come out of a certain change. The key is to not expend all your energy in avoiding the difficult parts of change. Instead, radically accept that the difficult parts are inevitable in the process of change. You might even see them as indicators that you are on the right path to your desired reality.

I know you've heard this analogy before, but do you think that the part where the caterpillar turns into a butterfly is filled with ease and excitement? There is definite pain and discomfort. The pain of breaking your current reality is a requirement for that break to happen in a clean way so you can achieve your desired change.

Do not allow pain to stop your progress. You can pause to feel that pain and listen to it. You can reflect on it, talk about it, and understand where it's coming from. Battle the resistance it's putting in your face with your internal resistance to going back to a state of stagnancy.

This next point will help with the part where you push through the pain.

2. Don't Take Hardship as a Sign of Moving in the Wrong Direction

You may have heard about "clean" and "dirty" pain. *Clean pain* is what we experience directly as a result of a painful event, whereas *dirty pain* is what we experience as a result of the thoughts and beliefs we ruminate on after the pain.

How does this apply to change? Clean pain would be a direct result of the change you chose to make. Say you decided to change your program in school. Clean pain would be the result of maybe having to pay an extra installment of tuition as a result of being in a new program, knowing that you won't see the same people you're used to seeing every day in your classes, knowing that the last X number of years kind of feels like it went to waste, knowing that now you have to spend more time in school than you anticipated, and so on. Dirty pain would be telling yourself things like, *See, you're a failure. You always make the wrong decision. All your friends are going to pity you for having to graduate a lot later than them. You don't know what you want to do in life.*

Think of going through a tough breakup. Clean pain is the inevitable pain you feel coming to terms with the fact that this relationship isn't for you, that you just spent months or years with someone, and now you have to start over. Clean pain deals with the facts. Dirty pain is when you take that ending and say, "This is just how my life is. Everyone ends up leaving me. I will never find someone. . . ."

Moral of the story is that clean pain is an essential and unavoidable part of everyday life that you need to feel in order to process your emotions, whereas dirty pain is not conducive to your progress in life. It just traps you and labels you.

I have absolutely no judgment when it comes to experiencing dirty pain, by the way. I went through that for much of my life, not knowing that a lot of my suffering was a direct result of my own thinking.

Don't blame yourself for your pain. Just because you can realize that a lot of your suffering is a direct result of your thinking, don't blame yourself for feeling that pain. You're human. Pain visits all of us, and the ability to feel it and allow it to be released is one of the healthiest things we can do. Walking around with unreleased pain that you refuse to feel will just burden you.

One of the most glorious days of your life will be when you realize that you have the power to change the narrative. And the way to do that is to change the narrator. Instead of the narrator being someone who conditioned you to see yourself or your life in a certain way, you become the narrator. Reclaiming the narrative of your story allows you to become aware of all the stories and plots you are part of unconsciously, to decide to no longer be a passive character in those stories and to decide to be the writer of your own tale.

Just as a plot develops over time, the same goes for your change. Think of a show such as *Friends*, for which the episode scripts are written as the show airs, based on the feedback from the audience and the natural progression they see. I watched an interview with the producers who said that they make changes on the spot in every episode as they are filming. If they were so stuck on the guarantee that an episode would go a certain way before they filmed it, there's no way the show would be as funny and satisfying. You have to be willing to see the power in the development of *your* plot as you are living it, not as a plan in advance.

It helps to be proactive when it comes to anticipating hardships along the way. For example, you may want to start waking up early every morning to go for a run. You know that for a while, your body is going to resist getting out of the comfy bed at a time when it's used to resting. So prepare to minimize your struggle to wake up. Maybe that means you go to bed early to train your body to wind down at an earlier time than it's used to. Maybe that means you set your alarm at a distance from the bed so that you are forced to get out of bed to turn it off. Maybe that means that you prepare the clothes you're going to wear for the run, with a bottle of water ready. That's a simple example, but being proactive applies to any other change in terms of helping you minimize the struggle you have with pushing forward. These are things within your control.

Say you're contemplating leaving a relationship of ten years. You know it's going to be hard. The uncertainty can be crippling, especially if there are children or any kind of shared asset involved. How can you be proactive in preparing for the messy, in-between part of getting to the other side of being in this relationship? This has to be customized, based on your knowledge of the things that hurt you the most. If your biggest fear is loneliness, you might want to start expanding your circle of support or start one altogether. If your biggest fear is knowing that you're going to face yourself, your truth, and your traumas, you might want to start seeing a therapist who can help you on your journey to discovering your childhood traumas and how they've shaped your view of yourself and the world. It might even help to keep a list of all the reasons you made your decision to leave so you can refer to it every time you feel your body gravitate toward your comfort and familiarity.

If you're contemplating a career change, being proactive could look like taking some time to research what you want to transition into. After that, you might need to look into required qualifications for such a position, whether there are openings in your desired area of living, what the standard salary for a job like that is and whether that will be enough for your lifestyle. Maybe you have to take on another job on top of it to compensate for any lost income. If you don't do any of this and just leave your current job, you might end up regretting your decision because it was hasty. Not only that, but you're also not setting yourself up for the best possible outcome, which for you is being in your career of choice.

Then there are changes we don't choose, like the ones discussed in chapter 3. The strategies in that chapter will help. However, you might find yourself wondering why it's taking you so long to just be okay with the change. You might find yourself saying things like, *Shouldn't I be okay by now? It's taking way too long for me to feel like my life is back to normal.* The truth is, you'd never say something like that about something you radically accept. Again, this is not to blame you for the way you're transitioning between realities, but simply to bring clarity to why the pain persists the way it does.

There's a story I shared in my last book, *Welcome Home*, about a situation with a guy I referred to as Noah. When he decided that he no longer wanted to communicate with me, I went down a path of self-exploration that led me to the root cause of my pain; my core belief that I didn't deserve love. In hindsight, that "rejection," which I now see as just an experience, offered me an opportunity to allow the pain of that core belief to be revealed to me. I then sat with it, understood how it formed by going back to my childhood experiences, and then I took the pens away from every person who shaped that belief about myself for me and started writing my story. For the longest time, I was consumed by the thought that someone as "smart, educated, and mature" as me shouldn't have held on to someone who clearly had no idea what he wanted. I wanted the past version of me who did that to go away. I wanted that memory erased from my mind. Every time it popped up, I'd feel immense discomfort and denial about how I acted.

The biggest revelation I had in going back to "normal" after a change I didn't choose is that I needed to stop rejecting myself by rejecting the part of me that experienced the pain. There was a part of me that was convinced that being at peace with what happened meant that I could erase that whole experience from my mind, that I just wouldn't think about it anymore. And the reason I was convinced by that was what going "back to normal" meant to me; not having that experience happen in the first place because it was not something I should've done.

Remember what we said about radical acceptance? The way I was handling this situation demonstrated the complete opposite of radical acceptance. It was actually radical rejection.

Your biggest indicator that you are finally okay with a change you didn't choose isn't your ability to erase it from your mind and never think of it again. It's when you are able to think about it and not want to push it away or change it. You can remind yourself that what happened is in the past, it cannot be changed, and it is part of your reality. You also have to stop judging the past version of you who went through that experience and the way that you reacted to it. You have to sit with that past self of yours with compassion and understanding. That's what that version of you needs, not judgment.

Of all the changes we don't choose, death holds a unique place in the trajectory of healing. Although my grandma passed away, there is still a part of me expecting to see her the next time I go to Lebanon. I don't think I'm rejecting reality; it's just difficult for me to imagine a reality without her. And I don't think there's anything wrong with that. There might never come a day when I think of the fact that she's no longer here and feel I'm totally okay with it. And that's not an indication of how healed or unhealed I am. With time, I will become better equipped to turn the sadness I feel into a way to love her even though she's not around.

If death happens to take someone you love, don't think that there should come a time when you are 100 percent okay with them being gone. There might always be an element of denial. And you shouldn't take that as a sign that something is wrong with you or with your way of dealing with their loss. Take it as an indication of how much you loved them and still love them. There will always be a space for them inside of your heart. And that's beautiful. On your journey of grief, you might find yourself going through moments where you feel intense happiness or joy of some sort and then you remember the person you lost and immediately feel guilty for feeling happy. That might pull you back into a more intense sadness at their memory. In moments like that, be gentle with yourself and allow yourself to miss them. Validate that you wish they could be part of this happiness with you. And remind yourself that any happiness you feel with them not around is not a betrayal of them or to the love that you have for them.

3. Give Your Body Time to Grow through the Change

Do you remember how we talked about honoring the choices that your body makes? On your journey of change, you will feel like you are being pulled back by your body to the original state you were in. And the farther you get from that original reality, the more real the change becomes. That can be both exciting and scary. When you attempt change that your body doesn't accept, you might feel an urge within to hold on to whatever it is that you are letting go or to be held by it. Here, I urge you to make the conscious choice to cut that cord that bonds you to what or who you're letting go, to be unanchored. You will go through moments when you will question whether that was the right thing for you to do, because if your normal, safe state was being anchored to something, the mere feeling of being unanchored will set off alarms of danger all over your body, which will scream, "Let's go back! Let's attach to something!"

When you've spent so much time trusting someone else with your life path, you will get to a point where you question whether you are qualified to make choices for yourself. You have to be willing to trust yourself. You have to be willing to give yourself a chance at leading your life. You have to open yourself up to taking risks and not judging your risk-taking based on its results. It's not the results that determine whether the change was worth it, but the growth you achieve as a result of trying for something.

In learning to trust myself, I noticed how much I struggled with putting into action what my mind knew reflected my self-worth. I would end up behaving like a child just wanting to be held, even if the price was leaving so much of what made me *me* behind. In healing this with my therapist, she taught me the following: Imagine a river. On one side, you would be living the way you are currently living (people-pleasing, self-abandoning, conditioned by your past upbringing, and so on); on the other side you'd be living in full authentic alignment with yourself. To get from one side to the other, you'll have to confront all that made you believe you need to be people-pleasing and self-abandoning. You'll understand that those patterns were part of what you were taught to do to keep your attachment to those you thought you couldn't survive without. This obviously begins with your relationship with your parents because you physically and emotionally depended on them for your survival. With time, your body doesn't recognize the difference between actually not being able to survive without certain patterns of behavior and *feeling* like you can't survive. That's why I always urge you to reflect on your childhood. What feels like a pull back into those old patterns is you getting stuck in doing what you normally did to survive. Though you might logically recognize that this behavior is bad for you, change is not as simple as recognizing. Your old patterns of survival will catch you like a strong current you feel you can't go against. You might feel like you have no control over your choices. You're just trying to survive. If you equate survival with approval, you might find yourself doing anything to make someone see you differently. If you equate survival with not wasting time, you will find yourself always looking for something to do. You know what your survival is. You know the patterns you fall into that you feel you're stuck in. Begin by acknowledging those patterns when you get caught in them. Then practice self-soothing and self-reliance and allow your current self to give your young, scared self what is needed. You are that protector for your younger self now.

Let's do a quick activity together. Take out a piece of paper. Write down these questions:

- Where are you now?
- Where do you want to go?
- What's standing in your way? (Reflecting back on the river analogy, what's in the middle of that river?)
- What can you do to get through each obstacle?

Here's an example of how these questions might be answered:

Where are you now?
I am in a state of being that requires people pleasing.

Where do you want to go?
I want to be in a state of having strong boundaries and putting myself first.

What's standing in your way? (Reflecting back on the river analogy, what's in the middle of that river?)
My childhood conditioning is standing in my way. It led me to believe that I am part of a collective. My individuality was never welcomed or celebrated. I always felt like it was selfish of me to think of myself.

What can you do to get through each obstacle?
Change my belief system about myself and the world: I matter. My individuality matters. My choices for myself matter.

Start practicing those new beliefs and dealing with the changes as they come up. Awareness of old patterns coming up will help me decide to self-soothe instead of going outward for validation.

Some of your supports might be people. But it's the supports you develop within you that will help in difficult moments. Becoming aware of your body is one support. For example, you're about to make a phone call, and you're really nervous. You find yourself doing anything to avoid making that call. That's a subconscious way your body is responding to a fear. You won't know what it is without going inward and seeking from your body the answer to the question, *What are you trying to tell me?*

A way to do this is to get into a comfortable position, close your eyes, and feel where the sensation of anxiety, fear, shakiness, and so on is in your body. Trying to do this on your own is huge. Because you are, in action, validating your body. You are saying, "I know you have wisdom within you that you are trying to guide me with."

Dr. Peter Levine refers to the obstacles in the middle of the river of healing as the trauma vortex, or there may be vortices. On your way from one side of the river (where you currently are) to the other side (where you are your most authentic, healed self) you will encounter the trauma(s) you've endured. Imagine a vortex structure—it's wider at the top and gets smaller and smaller as you go down. When you're caught by your traumas, or triggered, you spiral down the vortex. The lower you spiral, the fewer resources you have and the more you'll revert to survival mode strategies. Dr. Levine explains that the wider your support system is (whether that's friends, family, a therapist, and so on), which makes for a wider top of the vortex, the easier it will be for you to not get stuck in the vortex and spiral down to the tightest spot of the vortex, to a point of shutdown, where the feeling is so overwhelming that you feel you can't deal with it and just want to survive it. You ultimately get to the other side of the river when you are able to tap in to your trauma(s) in safe environments where you are seen, heard, and supported. Looking into the trauma(s) in your body will make you aware of your limiting beliefs, how you learned them, and how you can break through them into new beliefs formed by your authentic self. (For books that take an in-depth look at trauma, read *Waking the Tiger: Healing Trauma* by Peter A. Levine and Ann Frederick, *The Body Keeps the Score: Brain, Mind, and Body in the Healing of Trauma* by Bessel van der Kolk, *What Happened to*

You?: Conversations on Trauma, Resilience, and Healing by Bruce D. Perry, MD, PhD, and Oprah Winfrey, and *The Myth of Normal: Trauma, Illness & Healing in a Toxic Culture* by Gabor Maté, MD.)

Give your body time to catch up to your mind. And listen to your body instead of pressuring it through change. "I will go as fast as the slowest part of me feels safe" are words from a song called "Gentle With Myself" by Karen Drucker that my therapist shared with me. She told me to repeat those words every time I am hard on myself for not moving as fast as I think I should be going. What a beautiful affirmation.

4. Avoid Labeling Change as Good or Bad

Before a therapy appointment, I was preparing how I was going to start my conversation—"I have good news and bad news." My good news was that I was doing so much better in separating my pain from who I am. I was becoming the witness of pain, not the pain itself, every time it visits me. My bad news was that, in my practice of boundary setting, even though I'd gotten to a point where I could set the boundary firmly, I found myself slowly going back on it when I felt guilty.

Then I decided, based on all the work I'd been doing up to that point, that it didn't have to be good news or bad news. It was just news. Because the labeling of good and bad is all relative. It was interesting to me that I perceived my ability to separate myself from my pain as good and my difficulty with upholding boundaries as bad. Both were struggles of mine. But in the former area, I focused on the progress, whereas in the latter area I focused on the regression. In reality, I was making progress in both areas, and it was my perception that caused me to label one as good and one as bad. In the grand scheme of life, I was making incredible changes to the way I lived and the way I was unlearning, "unconditioning," and detaching myself from the image of the woman I was taught I needed to be.

I hope this encourages you to stop labeling your progress as good or bad. It is normal to have ups and downs on your way through a change of any sort. You might perceive a down as bad because you feel like you're going backward. But the reality could be that you took ten steps forward and two steps back. Taking two steps back doesn't mean that you are actually regressing. Going back to the example I just gave you, the fact that I was able to start setting boundaries in the first place when I was a people-pleaser for most of my life represented one hundred steps forward. My struggle with upholding a boundary didn't mean that I was regressing. It meant that I was moving forward and facing resistance from my deeply engrained patterning. That pattern showed up as guilt and shame any time I did or said something that caused another person to be uncomfortable or displeased with me. I was conditioned to believe that my assertion of my self—my wants, needs, values, likes, dislikes, and so on—automatically indicated that I was too much, a burden, and an inconvenience. The fact that I was struggling with carrying that guilt and shame opened the door for me to understand that they stemmed from my conditioning. So now, as I previously mentioned, any time I experience guilt or shame when I assert myself, the awareness I have about my conditioning allows me to ask, "Am I feeling guilty or shameful because I did something wrong or am I feeling guilty and shameful because I was conditioned to believe that my authentic self was wrong?"

As you go through your journey of change, be mindful of the moments you are hard on yourself because you weren't able to keep a promise you made to yourself. Take this as an opportunity to approach this changing, in-between self of yours with immense compassion and friendship. Be for yourself what you needed when everyone else was being hard on you, and you were echoing their voices. Make the conscious choice to no longer echo the voices around you, whether they are positive or negative. You are not an echo. You are a powerful, confident, and self-trusting roar. You know how to speak to yourself with utmost empathy and compassion. You know when to hold yourself accountable in the most constructive ways. And you know when to conserve your energy and choose silence in the face of chaos.

You have the power to define what happens around you and to you with whatever words you choose. And I hope the words you choose are ones that reflect your understanding that everything in life is an experience. When you look at it abstractly and without context, you might very well describe it as bad or negative. But when you look at it in the grand scheme of things, you can tell yourself, "The fact that this is what I'm struggling with, when a few months ago or a few years ago, I wasn't even aware that this was something I needed to work on, is a blessing. The fact that I am struggling with this means that I am pushing up against something as I move forward toward my most authentic life."

5. Don't Judge the Journey by Its Destination

Every moment of your life has the potential to be a moment of learning. Even the moments you choose to do nothing at all can be moments of learning. I used to feel so guilty and unproductive when I would spend any amount of time not doing something productive, especially if it involved watching television, scrolling through my phone, or going out for dinner with friends, when I knew that I could be doing more work. I used to look at moments like that and think, *What a waste of time. I could be doing something that actually causes progress in my life and is an investment in me and my future.* I only perceived those things as a waste of time because of my conditioning that my well-being was dependent on what I did. So naturally any time I spent *not doing*, I perceived as indications that I wasn't okay.

I genuinely believe it's the reason that I don't have many close friendships and why I don't know how to just go out and have fun. Do you remember when I told you about my dance lessons? How I always told myself I'm just not someone who dances? Well, that belief was a result of this same conditioning.

My only sources of relaxation or resetting were sleep and spending time with my nieces and nephews. In hindsight, spending time with them was subconsciously a way to give my inner child what I believed she needed. Seeing the pure joy and happiness on their faces from just running around and being silly, being held, and being made to laugh were all things I felt deprived of in my childhood. I was deprived of feeling special and integral to the lives of those around me. Maybe those moments felt like rest because they healed my inner child.

The older I become, the more apparent it is that sleep and spending time with people I love aren't sufficient to meet my needs for rest. There has to be an element of rest that has absolutely nothing to do with *doing* and everything to do with *being*. Most of us don't even know who we are, and that's why we avoid moments of being that self of ours: "How do I just *be* myself when I don't *know* myself?"

I used to consider it a badge of honor to be called a hard worker, someone who was always available to help and support, someone who was so determined and accomplished. Now, I know that when I am called those things, it is coming at the expense of my peace. Yes, I am a hard worker. But I don't want to be the kind of hard worker who never takes a break, eats while she is continuing a task, and always multitasks. I want to be someone who can focus on one thing at a time—even if it's only for fifteen minutes—and then jumps to another task and another and so on. I want to be someone who doesn't carry the weight of everything that needs to be done while I'm doing just one thing.

Yes, I love to help and support those around me. But I don't want to be someone who does that at the expense of things that need to be done for myself. Yes, I am someone who is determined and accomplished. But I don't want that to be all I define myself by. I want to be able to look at this self of mine who isn't doing anything and see her as equally worthy and okay.

Trust me, happiness isn't built out of titles, accomplishments, milestones, money, possessions, or status. When you're working so hard, ask yourself, "Is your effort driven by your quest to live a life of choice and authenticity?" If your work is aligned with your authenticity, your focus can stay on the present moment. That's because your destination is already here, with you, right now. It's you—your authentic truth and your authentic life.

When I graduated from my doctorate program, someone asked me what doors this degree would open for me. And it took me down a spiral of thinking, *Oh my, was this a waste of time? I don't need this degree to teach anywhere. I only need it if I want to be a professor one day, and I'm really not interested in that.* Like, would this degree only be worth it if it gets me to a place that gives me a new title or more money? Those three full years of hard work were ones that I spent learning, researching, and building connections with my colleagues. Those three years were full of investing my time in something that I loved and enjoyed so much. Those three years were full of moments when I proved to myself over and over again that I had the ability to choose how I spent my time. I showed myself how capable I was of disciplining myself. Now that I have this degree, even if I never work with it, would I say that those three years were a waste?

Absolutely not. If my only goal with this degree was to get a job with it, then I might have perceived it as a waste of time. But if my focus was on everything I learned along the way, the limits to which I pushed my thinking, the ways I challenged myself to think critically about different topics and pushed myself to express myself in different ways, then none of that was a waste of time. The times when I didn't do as well as I knew I could have if I had invested more in certain assignments or tasks taught me that it's okay to not be perfect. And it's okay to decide that you are only capable of putting 80 percent of the energy and investment that you normally could because of all the other circumstances in your life. That shows strength, not laziness, lack of determination, or lack of hard work.

I once went into business with people who overpromised and underdelivered. I paid them upward of $30,000 to create content that they promised would be shared on different platforms to help my message get out into the world. They promised that their plans for my brand would help me bring in upward of $100,000 a month, even though that's not what I approached them with or expected of them. Instead, what I was going for was ensuring that more people around the world had access to my work on platforms they already followed. A few months into our partnership, I realized that all the promises and words I was fed were not true. And it was heartbreaking for me because I truly respected them as people and didn't think that this would

happen. This was early on in my writing career, and I was learning the hard lesson that sometimes people will approach you and
make great promises because they want to deliver on promises
they made to themselves for the amount of money they wanted
to make per year. I went through moments when I would reflect
on this experience and think, *I was such an idiot to believe that
something like that could happen. I should have been more assertive
with my expectations throughout our collaboration. What a waste of
time. What a waste of money.* But you know, the best thing that
came out of this collaboration was being introduced to Stephan,
who is one of my closest friends and biggest cheerleaders in my
life. Had I not gone through that experience with those guys,
there was no way I would have been introduced to him and developed this friendship with him. To me, meeting him on that
journey was worth it even though the destination of that journey didn't happen.

Sometimes destinations that we aim for but don't reach
prove themselves to be dead ends that we thankfully avoided.
Or didn't see as *the end* of the journey. What we might think is
the destination that is best for us sometimes reveals itself as a
shiny beautiful thing that we thought would make our lives better only to realize it was an illusion with no real substance. We
could look at our inability to reach that destination as a failure
or a waste of time, or we could look at all the things we learned
along the journey to get to that destination and see those things
as enough, as worth it.

I also want to give you an example related to relationships. A lot of the times when we aim to be in a relationship, it's because we are hoping that someone will take away our inner pain. That someone will just fill a void we feel inside. That void could be missing a past partner or feeling like we are not good enough just because someone else isn't choosing us. That void could be our belief that we will never have our happily ever after.

Take a moment to be honest with yourself about what that void is.

We get into a relationship and, for the first while, it feels like all of our problems are solved or can be overcome because of the dopamine rush we get as a result of finally being with someone. But bit by bit, reality starts to reveal itself. No amount of love by someone else will replace the love we need to pour into ourselves. A lot of times, instead of coming to terms with that, we focus on the disappointment that we experience as a result of not reaching that happily-ever-after destination. In my view, the awareness you gain through a relationship about the things that hurt and trigger you the most, learning about the importance of expressing yourself and your needs, learning about the things that stand in the way of setting your boundaries and upholding them, learning that it is okay to decide that someone you love deeply isn't the right person for you—all of that is a learning experience about yourself that will bring you closer to your authentic truth. If you simply look at the time you spent with this experience as a waste because it didn't lead you to that happily-ever-after destination you initially aimed for, you miss out on truly learning about yourself.

Just like you hear "don't judge a book by its cover," don't judge a journey by its destination. And don't let an unreached destination fool you into believing the journey was time wasted. Or that it's an indication that you're back at square one. You can choose to continue past an unreached destination because it proved itself to you to be one more learning experience.

Do you remember what your life was like ten years ago? Where were you living? What were the things you enjoyed doing? What were the things you wanted to change? And where did you see yourself in ten years? Does your current life look like what you thought you would have? If your life does embody where you pictured yourself, reflect on the mindset you had regarding change and use that approach to pursue new changes in your life. If your current situation doesn't resemble where you thought you would be, follow up with a list of people and things you are grateful for over those ten years; because those wouldn't exist without your life going exactly the way it went. Change does not always occur as expected. In fact, it rarely ever happens exactly as expected. And maybe the secret to navigating the uncertainty that comes with change is for us to trust in our ability to live through it and make the best of it. Yes, uncertainty opens the door for something to happen that is worse than what we hope for. It is also uncertainty that opens up the possibility of something better than what we hope for.

CHAPTER 7

Propellers of Change

H ave you ever heard the story about the dog and rusty nail? I don't know who told it originally, but my friend Stephan shared it with me.

A little boy was sitting with his grandpa and his dog outside. Every couple of minutes, the dog lets out a howl. The boy could tell he was in pain. After a few howls, the boy finally asked his grandpa, "Is he okay?"

"Yes," replied the grandpa. "He's just sitting on a rusty nail."

"Why doesn't he get up?" the boy questioned.

"Because the pain isn't painful enough," his grandpa answered.

Maybe the pain of staying where you are is not painful enough to be unbearable. Maybe you can survive through it. Maybe you've adapted. But maybe you're just afraid of what will happen when you do get up. Maybe you don't think you can get off the rusty nail and heal. The moral of the story is that what propels you to change might be that the pain of staying where you are is too unbearable. And what propels you to change might be that the promise of change is more exciting than where you are now. Reflect on changes you've made in your life and identify what your motivators were. Grab a journal and reflect on this if necessary. What is it that gets you up, ready to go for the change you need or want to make? What is it that, perhaps years after recognizing you need to change, gets you moving on it?

After my friend Jen left her twenty-five-year marriage, I asked her how she did it. How did she go from being with someone for so many years, sharing everything, to living on her own, starting over? She told me that when the pain of staying as you are becomes bigger than the pain of losing whatever it is that kept you in your place, you will be propelled to change. But do you want to be motivated by pain or do you want to be motivated by what you want? Perhaps the biggest impetus of change is realizing that your life is yours and yours only. Living anything outside of your authentic truth is a waste of time. A waste of life.

My sister once told me that I should live my life by my rules. She's fifteen years older than I am. She said, "I wish I lived my life the way I wanted, based on what I knew was right for me. Now, when I look back at all the years I wasted trying to be what others wanted me to be, I'm filled with so much regret. I let myself down. I did what everyone else wanted me to do and left my own wants behind. It's too late for me to live how I want to live; I don't have that time or energy now."

While it might be better to go for certain changes at a specific period in your life, the time that you are *ready* to make that change is ultimately the optimal time for you. Your life is unique. All the learnings you have obtained are specific to you, based on what you went through and what experience you accumulated over time. You have to start seeing your story and how it should be lived through your eyes, through your actions.

I'm not going to give you a lecture on what will prompt you to change. You have to figure that out for yourself. Does the push come from the inside or out? Are you intrinsically or extrinsically motivated? Figure that out, then decide where you want your motivation to be directed. Do you want to be led by others or do you want to lead yourself? I hope you will see the value in leading yourself.

What propels you to change will always be very personal to you. I've seen people decide to change after enduring a very minor incident. Sometimes all you need is a moment that, from the outside looking in, doesn't seem cataclysmic. It can be a simple thing, like your partner not making your birthday special but throwing a party for a friend on that person's birthday, or a co-worker being recognized for work that you did. Sometimes it's at the point when you've just had enough of staying as you are. There is an end to the patience you have. You don't know when that is. It just comes. It happens when it happens. You just have to let it. But remember that you don't have to wait until something forces you to change—you can make the decision to empower yourself.

Here are ways to propel change in your life:

1. Make Room in Your Life for Change

An empty space calls to be filled. A filled space doesn't need anything new. The same goes for the life you're living. If you truly want to effect change in your life, you have to make room for it. You have to be willing to create space for the new by letting go of the old.

You make room in your life when you remove the clutter that's occupying your time and energy. But it's not only about making room, it's also about teaching you to be okay with letting go, no matter how long you held on. Maybe that's the hardest part, the letting go. Letting go shows that you can live without what you thought you needed to survive. This is not just about things (although we'll get to that), but also about mindsets, emotions, thoughts, and people. Let's begin with internal decluttering.

YOUR INNER ENVIRONMENT NEEDS DECLUTTERING

I tend to declutter my surroundings when I feel like I really need to focus on the work at hand. I feel like I can't focus unless I make sure that nothing around me is out of place or unnecessary. I used to see this "need" as a positive step toward living a life of simplicity and minimalism. Then one day, as I did my daily routine of getting my external surroundings as perfect as possible so that I could start writing, I heard this voice inside of me that said, *I need to be organized too.* And I thought to myself, *Wow. I've actually never taken the time to look at the metaphorical mess within me and decide what needs to be thrown out, tended to, cleaned, put in an appropriate place, and so on.* I realized that I was putting all my energy into decluttering and organizing my external environment when my actual need was to declutter my *inner* world. I was mistaken in assuming that my external environment would dramatically affect my internal world. Do you see what I just did there? What I had labeled as progress, I suddenly saw as a mistake. But really, it was just an *assumption* that I needed to examine further.

Here are some steps you can use to start the process of becoming aware of your inner environment.

1. **Pause:** Take a moment to go inward and ask yourself, *What emotion am I feeling right now? What thought or sensation is present?*

2. **Sit with "it" (thought, emotion, sensation, and so on):** Instead of pushing the emotion or thought away, distracting yourself, or talking yourself out of how important it is, sit with it and ask, *How does this feel in my body? What is it trying to tell me?*

3. **Remember that you are not "it":** You are the seer, the manager of that emotion, thought, or sensation. Don't aim to control it. Aim to understand it. Listen to what it's

telling you about yourself and separate that from who you are.

4. **Make space for a new "it":** Don't spend all your time stuck in the same loop of having a thought or emotion, identifying with it as if it is your truth, and leaving it unheard or unresolved. As the seer and manager of your inner environment, decide what you will do with it. Once you learn what it wants to tell you, give yourself permission to open yourself up to new thoughts and emotions you can experience.

5. **Forgive yourself:** Sometimes we get stuck because we keep replaying the same memories in our minds and beat ourselves up over what we should have done differently. We judge ourselves for not doing what we now know would've been the best thing to do. Accept the past fully, including past versions of yourself that were just trying to survive. Let go of how it should have been.

Not only will emotional decluttering allow you to make space within you for new emotions and thoughts, but it will also give you power after realizing that you are not the thoughts and emotions that visit you. You may have believed that they are integral to your identity because they've been visiting you for so long. You may have mistaken them for permanent residents inside of you. But the truth is, they kept visiting you because they were looking for a resolution—and that resolution will begin with your awareness, validation, understanding, and release of them. If you shut them out or judge yourself for having them, they will stick around, searching for validation.

These recurring thoughts and emotions make us feel stuck and stagnant. Let's say that from a young age, one of your parents always put you down and told you that you'll never amount to anything in life. If you find a voice in your mind repeating itself on a daily basis saying, *you will never amount to anything*, it's not enough to tell yourself that you logically know that's not true. It is *essential* for you to decondition your body from that narrative. That on its own is decluttering.

You are decluttering the noises in your body that are holding you to an old narrative, one that you had no tools to change when you were younger. Practically speaking, when you hear that voice inside of you, you might say, *It's interesting that this voice that is not mine and that has nothing to do with me is still here. I recognize that it's from my past conditioning. I also recognize that it doesn't speak to my current truth or the truth that I want to continue living.* This process on its own allows you to stop operating through your subconscious and unconscious beliefs about yourself and start operating through your conscious understanding of who you really are. It will also allow you to have a different view of yourself, or to rebrand yourself, in your mind. If you always told yourself, *I am just a very sensitive person who cares too much to the point where I can't set boundaries because I can't handle letting people down*, then you are limiting yourself based on your conditioning. You have the power to rebrand yourself and say, *I am a sensitive person, and that means that I'm responsible for conserving my energy and making sure that I don't say yes when I really want to say no. I can set boundaries with people. I am working on changing the conditioning that tells me that it is my responsibility to manage and soothe the emotions of those around me as a result of choices I make for myself.*

If the image you have of yourself is *I am too serious to be silly and have fun*, then you will perceive every action of yours that isn't spent doing productive work as a waste. You will judge yourself for putting yourself in settings where you are just enjoying your time with no end goal other than that. If you were to rebrand yourself and say, *I tend to be serious most of the time, but I also can be fun and playful when I want to*, that would allow you to let go of taking things seriously all the time. It would also remove the judgment you have toward yourself any time you're not being productive.

Do you see how this internal decluttering allows you to be aware of all that has been living rent-free inside of you, releasing it, and introducing new thoughts, emotions, and ways of viewing yourself and the world around you?

Stop basing the goodness of the experiences within you on the goodness of the experiences outside of you. Instead, learn to be a listener to everything that happens inside of you. Only then can you be the most powerful force of change in your own life. When you're in the middle of a life change, remember the change is *for* you and *about* you. As you're making this change, you are changing as a person. It's not only the end goal that will determine whether you can label this change as good or bad. As long as this change is bringing you closer to figuring out who you authentically are and what your authentic life looks like, it's good change.

My tendency to clear out and organize my physical environment before I started focusing on my work was really about maintaining a sense of control in my life because my inner world felt so chaotic—this was an important realization for me. But it's not as simple as that. I also learned over time that what we keep in our physical environment is very telling about our inner patterns as well.

YOUR PHYSICAL ENVIRONMENT REFLECTS YOUR INNER ENVIRONMENT

The first time in my life that I visited Canada was with my mom. I was six years old. My brothers and sisters started making their way to Canada when I was around four years old. By the time I was thirteen, all of them were permanently living in Canada. I stayed with my dad in Lebanon for the most part. Because my mom would travel back and forth, that left me for several periods of time living with different relatives. When I was thirteen, I traveled to Canada for the summer because it was my sister's wedding. I stayed for a couple months and returned to Lebanon alone. My mom had bought a chocolate bar to donate to some charity, but she gave it to me when I left just in case I felt like eating it on the way back. I remember keeping that chocolate bar with me as long as I possibly could. I would eat a little piece here and there to feel like my mom was around.

This wasn't the first time I did something like this. Anytime my brothers visited from Canada, they brought me chocolates because one of them worked at Nestlé. I held on to those chocolates like they lasted forever. And I remember being very aware that the reason I held on to them so tightly was that they made me feel like my brothers were there.

This pattern of holding on to things that in the grand scheme of life had no meaning or value continued into my adulthood. The littlest of things became sentimental to me. The wrapper of a chocolate that I ate at an event that made me feel some kind of way, pieces of clothing I was handed down from my sister, movie stubs, and so on. It didn't matter what the value was; to me, holding on to an object that reminded me of someone showing me love by offering me something was the value.

And I didn't just do that with objects. I did it with moments in time too.

After I permanently moved to Canada at the age of sixteen, my brothers built a new house for all of us to live in, my parents included. Years later, I have a vivid memory of waking up one wintery morning when the snow was falling heavily. Usually, I dreaded mornings like that because it meant I had to go outside and clean my car before I headed to the school where I taught. But that morning, as I was about to walk out the door, my brother walked in with two coffees in his hand. He gave me one and said, "I cleaned your car and turned it on for you so it could heat up. All you have to do is get in it and go to school."

Even though at the time I was twenty-two years old, I still remember exactly how overwhelmed with emotion I was in that moment. All of a sudden, I wasn't feeling alone or lonely anymore. I felt cared for and taken care of, two things I ached for my whole life. I felt so grateful that my brother thought of me in that way and that he took time out of his morning to make sure I had an easier morning myself.

I know you might be reading this and thinking, *It's just coffee! It's not a big deal. It doesn't mean anything.* To me, it meant the world. I still hold on to that moment to this day.

In hindsight, memories such as this make it very clear to me the reason that I hold onto people, emotions, and things is because I isolate moments of connection and just want to lock them somewhere so they never go away. Because those moments were so rare, I never wanted them to change. This explained to me why I had a hard time accepting that, for example, someone who once had feelings for me could stop having those feelings. I would be so stuck on the moments when I felt like they had feelings for me that I couldn't come to accept any change. Even though on a logical level, I understand that people grow through time and that moments of feeling love toward others aren't eternal, my body had a hard time accepting the possibility of that reality. I did not want to let go of any connection I felt. The desperation that bred in me was embarrassing. Even worse, the lack of boundaries that bred in me was self-destructive. When you're so malnourished for love and connection, the last thing you think about when you receive it is whether it's healthy, unconditional, or real. You don't have time to think of what your expectations are because your only expectation is that you will get a rare moment of connection.

Unfortunately, there are people in the world who sense your need for love and take advantage of it to gain medicine for their own pain and to get their wants and needs met.

You might be wondering why I'm telling you this. What does this have to do with making room for change? The things we ache for most in life are the underlying drivers for everything we do. Even though the change you are trying to achieve on the surface may feel like it has absolutely nothing to do with your core needs, it is most likely subconsciously driven by them. Maybe you want to prove yourself to someone. Maybe you want to prove your worth in a way that you have been taught would make you worthy. Maybe you are running away from your core beliefs about yourself by trying to achieve something externally that proves those beliefs wrong.

Take a moment to be honest with yourself. Reflect on the change that you are currently trying to make and ask yourself, *why am I trying to make this change?*

It is so essential for you to be aware of the recurring patterns of thinking and feeling that your inner environment engages in so you can make sure they are not extending the space they take up emotionally. That space could be occupied with new thoughts, emotions, and surroundings.

For you to be able to make the change you want in your life, you must make sure not only that you are aware of the inner patterns but also that you put yourself in a physical environment that best supports your change, one that reflects your decluttered inner environment.

YOUR PHYSICAL ENVIRONMENT NEEDS DECLUTTERING

Don't put yourself in an environment that constantly devalues you and triggers you to prove yourself or your worth in some way. In a devaluing environment, you may find yourself trying to change the opinions of those around you, or trying to reason with them and show them that you really aren't worthy of that devaluation. So many of us get stuck in these kinds of situations. And just as decluttering your desk doesn't always organize your emotions, changing your inner environment doesn't always make the external one better. Yes, working on yourself on the inside is intrinsically good and has the potential to positively impact how you operate in the world, but that's not always enough. Not every situation has the capacity to nourish and nurture your inner environment.

I needed to start looking at my physical environment as a combination of all the things that mean something to me and serve a purpose for me, as opposed to a culmination of all the things I was able to attain or gather over time. This allowed me to build a physical environment of choice, instead of a physical environment of things I'm afraid to let go of because of the energy I put into attaining them, or because they were given to me and represent a moment of care or connection.

Another thing that I was able to see was that I have the right to be selective in the things I accept into my space. Instead of just feeling obligated to keep what I am given, I can choose to be grateful to be given something and choose that I don't want it in my space. And when it comes to things that I get for myself, I have the right to outgrow what I once worked really hard for and once desired. It doesn't matter how much money I paid or how much time and energy I put into attaining it, the fact that it is only taking up space because I'm hoping to use it one day or because I'm feeling guilty about investing in something that just no longer adds value in my life, is enough reason to let it go.

I realized that there are people in my life who aren't good for me. I realized that I no longer have to hold on to people just because of how long they've been in my life or because of the potential of what they could be one day or because of who they were. I realized that I no longer have to keep people in my life just because they are nice and kind and I don't have a reason to say, *I want you out of my life.* I realized that I don't have to accept someone's love just because I need love. I have the right to be selective with whose love is good for *me.* I realized that just because a person is a good person, and they have good manners and values, it doesn't make me a bad person to say, *This is not the right person for me.* I also realized it's toxic for me to keep people as placeholders in my life until the right people come along.

The same kind of mentality can be applied to careers and money. Just because a certain job pays you a certain amount of money doesn't mean that you must stay in it. Maybe there's another job out there that will bring you inner peace. If you are sacrificing what feels authentic to you just for money, you'll probably end up using much of that money to either numb or heal the pain of working in a way that isn't authentic to you. Just because a certain job offers you security for life, it doesn't mean that you have to choose it over a job that makes you feel alive, purposeful, and happy.

Your ability to look at your physical environment as one that you are able to change for yourself based on your conscious choices will give you so much power and autonomy over other choices in your life.

Once I became aware of this power, I found myself becoming hyperaware of every object in my physical environment. Things that I held on to for so long became easy for me to either discard, offer to someone who I knew actually needed them, or give as a donation. Eventually I reached the most sacred space of possessions, my closet. I was shocked at how quickly I was able to let go of pieces of clothing I held on to for so long because I imagined how good they would look when I wore them or how good they would look if I could pair them with something else I could buy. I was shocked at how quickly I was able to let go of pieces I held on to because of how much money I paid for them.

And instead of doing it all in one day, which would have

been really overwhelming for me, I challenged myself to start a pile in a corner in my room. Every day, I would take five pieces of clothing that I hadn't worn in a long time and that I knew I was only keeping because of the value invested in them or the potential I believed they had. I'd ask myself, would I wear this piece right now? And if the answer was no, that eased my letting go of it. Obviously, this didn't apply to outfits that are appropriate to certain occasions, like weddings, parties, or public speaking events. I'm talking about everyday clothes.

Going through the drawers in my washrooms, the cupboards in my kitchen, my coats and shoes—I took out so many things that I knew other people in my life actually have uses for—I created a lot of space for intentional additions.

This approach offers a holistic revolution to your life. It not only allows you to let go of material possessions but also changes your view of the people you keep in your circle just because of how long they've been there or because they know so much about you, and so on. You know the reasons.

It is necessary to declutter your space internally and externally of things that were chosen for you and things that your inauthentic, conditioned self chose, and things for which you no longer have a use. This will open space for your authentic, conscious, unconditioned self to make choices.

Developing the mindset that everything you keep around you and within you will serve a purpose for you revolutionizes your sense of leadership over your life. Even if the role it serves is that it brings you joy or peace, that's enough.

2. Don't Be Afraid to Ask for Help When You Need It

Being strong doesn't mean you have to do it alone. Know that there are people who want to help you make positive changes in your life. I understand why you might believe otherwise. If the only people you're close with are people who don't believe in you in the way you need them to or who don't accept you, then you'll have to make your change without those individuals. When we depend on people and they let us down, and it happens over and over, we might develop the belief that trusting people will always lead to negative results. But take the time to build connections with others. You'll meet people who have gone through a similar transition or who are currently going through it. I mean, you and I met at a certain point.

Don't fall into the trap of believing that it's better to be alone and do things on your own than it is to bring people in on your change and seek help from them. Although the amount of strength you gain by doing what you once thought was impossible—doing it alone—will boost your confidence and prove that the fear of being alone is actually something you can survive, have no doubt that the part of you that believes this is only aiming to protect you. The fear remembers what you experienced in the past when you let people in on your change or when you asked for help and felt let down.

It's helpful to differentiate between asking for help in general and asking for help from the right people. The best way to identify someone who is right for you is to consider, *Do they have my best interests in mind?* You'll find that those who do will always honor you where you are. They won't try to shame or pressure you into doing what you're not comfortable doing or what doesn't resemble you. They won't think of how your actions reflect on them. They meet you where you are, exactly the way you need to be met. While you may have been scarred by asking for help from the wrong people, trust that there are people out there who will honor your request and offer you the exact kind of support you need.

Asking for help not only demonstrates your openness to trusting people. It also demonstrates your trust in yourself. You trust that your need for support is not too much, that it's a natural part of being human. Yes, sometimes others see what is best for us, but those who have *our* best interest in mind never shame us for the pace at which we're moving. They never make our inability to do what we know we need to do mean something about us. They understand that there is some belief or pain within us that's making us feel that we're not able to make the change we know we want to make. Think of who those people are for you. Take a moment to express gratitude for having them in your life.

3. Be the Center of Your Attention

How often were you made to feel selfish because you thought of yourself first? It's a dangerous message many of us are given from a young age, especially those of us who grew up in a family where enmeshment is the dynamic that holds the family together. It will be hard for you to consider putting yourself first because that requires you to consider how everyone else will feel and think about your choice before you make it.

We are changing that here.

You are no longer a puzzle piece that only fits when you cut off parts of yourself. You are now the whole puzzle! You fit into *your* world. All your parts are holistically working together to make you feel like you belong within yourself; as in, you are okay to move forward with your plans without the approval of others.

You are the center of attention in this world of yours. You are not simply on the periphery or margin, only adding commentary, suggestions, or clarifications here and there. You are in the center of the page. You are what the book of your life is about! Stop making yourself small by not wanting to cause too much noise. If that "noise" is your voice, who you are, and what you want for yourself, then be noisy. Be loud. The discomfort of others with your change is not on you to deal with or change. It's for them to deal with.

With any change you contemplate making, put yourself at the center of that change. Even if this change is meant to help you add more value to the world around you, it must be centered on you. It will be driven by you, so what's the problem with it being centered on you?

If you find that you aren't fitting into the puzzle of the world around you, say to yourself, "I don't want to be part of this puzzle anymore." The urge to be part of it will make you change yourself to fit in, not belong, and you will get stuck in a loop of wanting that puzzle to change and dwelling on why it's not. I'm sure you've heard that you can't *change the people* around you, but you can change *the people around you*. And what propels that change is you and your conviction that the most important thing in this world of yours is that you allow yourself to live a life that is most authentic to you. A life that is not based on other people's opinions, no matter who they are. A life that isn't most externally peaceful when you hide parts of you or hold them back from their full potential. If your internal drive to make change for yourself causes chaos around you, it is not your inside you have to change or filter, but the outside.

Being the center of your attention will allow you to tune in to your body in a way that highlights the messages it's trying to send you. It could be that you have unresolved thoughts and emotions from the past that keep visiting you. What are the recurring thoughts and emotions that consume you for a certain period? You go through this cycle almost every single day, and it's never resolved and put to rest. Write down those recurring thoughts and emotions. The mere awareness of them will initiate the process of resolving them. And it's not just a resolution that you will reach. You will also learn lessons about yourself, why you behave in certain ways, and how much power you actually have.

Let's say you are constantly reliving a certain memory, one that left you with some kind of trauma. Now remember that the trauma isn't what happened to you but what happened inside of you as a reaction to what happened to you. This doesn't mean that you are to blame for your reaction. It's meant to validate that how something affects you is out of your control. What is within your control is deciding to allow yourself to be the teller of the story of what happened and how it affected you. What is within your control is trying to give yourself the compassion you would give someone you love in a moment like that. What is within your control is to work on developing tools to help you navigate your triggers and where they lead. Often when a traumatic event or memory is too overwhelming, we avoid going back to it at any cost. That's why you might be dissuaded from seeking therapy, because you can't imagine speaking about something so overwhelming for a whole hour. In his book *What Happened to You?*, author Dr. Bruce Perry makes it very clear that sometimes a person can only spend a minute or two talking about an experience, and they shouldn't be pushed to spend more time than they are able without getting severely activated. The ability to talk about something for a minute or two, leaving it for a while and coming back to it when we feel like we are ready to talk about it again, even if it is also for another few minutes, is what allows that trauma to be seen and validated over time.

Being the center of your attention means you ask yourself,

What should have happened to you but didn't? Those are traumas too. Uncovering them will wake you to the limits that have been placed on you. For example, if you weren't given positive feedback when you were younger, you might have developed a way of being that is heavily fixated on external validation because it felt good, so that's what you valued. That's what shaped your view of the world. That's what shaped for you what's right, what's wrong, what's allowed, and what's not allowed. Bringing all of this into your awareness will allow you to understand why you make others' feedback the center of your attention. And that begins the process of you coming back to being that center for yourself.

Being the center of your attention means that you trust your intuition. You trust yourself. You check in with yourself and how you feel about your progress before you check in with others. You also take responsibility instead of blaming others for the way you are progressing. And in situations where others are negatively affecting your progress, you can firmly set boundaries that don't just aim to protect you from others' violations but that treat every part of you with the love, respect, and worthiness you deserve.

4. See Yourself as the Leader of Your Life

Have you ever been in a situation where you felt like all you needed was a hug? What happened if you didn't get one? Imagine putting your arms around yourself, giving yourself a hug, and saying all the words you wanted to hear from someone else. That is one of the most difficult things you'll ever have to do. Try looking at yourself in the mirror in the morning and telling yourself, *I love you. I believe in you.* And see the power it has. Your struggle to say something like that to yourself or to give yourself a hug or the comfort that you need from others shows you how you might subconsciously not believe that you deserve any of those things because of your conditioning. Uncovering that will allow you to change it.

In the process of making any change in your life, you must see yourself as the leader of your life. And a leader doesn't just make decisions. A leader also tends to the needs of those they are leading. You have to give yourself what you need, especially when the people around you only meet your needs when you conform to how they want you to be.

Remember the ship analogy we used when we talked about living your most authentic life? Well, here you are seeing yourself as the captain of that ship of your life. Perhaps after diving into the ocean of your authenticity and tasting the sweetness of living an authentic life, you will decide to build a ship for yourself and throw the survival mode ship away. This ship has no conditions for being welcome on it. It has no limits to where you can go. It is not controlled by all the fears you have. And it has no holes at the bottom.

On this ship, you are the one who makes decisions about which direction to take. You are also the one responsible for making sure it's well maintained. You figure out what you need and how to get it. You are the one who gets to decide who is allowed aboard and who's not.

Having this amount of power comes with a big responsibility as well. You take responsibility for your decisions and make changes accordingly. You also give yourself the opportunity to take risks, for example, by heading to unknown destinations, while being fully aware your choice might lead you to dead ends or places from which you have to detour. And that's all part of your understanding and acceptance that the effectiveness of your leading your life is not dependent on whether you get to where you initially intended, but on the journey and what you learn along the way. Even if you learned nothing at all, how would you have known before you tried?

Being the leader of your life means that you will inevitably make mistakes. You will fall short of your expectations on some days. And that's okay. What matters most is that you are honest with yourself, compassionately, in moments like that. Give yourself the grace you so easily give to others when they let you down in some way. You are human too.

Seeing yourself as the leader of your life will propel your change because you are not waiting on someone to change your life. You understand that you are the one you've been waiting for.

Being the leader of your life tasks you with a big responsibility: setting boundaries. Boundaries are focused on you. They stem from you. They are for you and about you. They do not aim to change other people's behavior. Rather, they aim to express what you are okay and not okay with, what you are comfortable and not comfortable with, what your needs and limits are, and so on. As the leader of your life, you are the one in charge of your energy and where it's allocated. You are also in charge of replenishing it. Wasting your energy on trying to change people's behavior is a very expensive price to pay. Your energy should not extend past expressing what you'll accept or not. What others choose to do is not an indication of the success of the boundaries you set. Their choice is your indicator for what your next step will be. Will you have to reinstate your boundary with more assertion? Or will you have to limit your contact with this person? You must do what is best for you, what shows that *you* value your energy, worth, and time.

In *Welcome Home*, I talk about boundaries being something you build over time. I advise against forcing yourself to start setting boundaries without going through the process of understanding why you've struggled with setting them for so long. The reason I advise against it is that you are taking the risk of going back on your boundary the moment you experience what used to deter you from setting them in the first place. It could be shame, guilt, feeling excluded, being accused of being selfish, or being treated passive-aggressively as if you did something wrong, among other things. These are very uncomfortable emotions and consequences to deal with, so we often go back on the boundary to avoid them.

Setting a boundary doesn't have to be complicated. You don't have to explain or overexplain yourself for it to be valid. It could be as simple as:

No.

I will only come for dinner if you give me your word that you will not talk to me about X topic.

I am not okay with your liking provocative pictures on social media.

I will do the following chores, and I need you to do X, Y, Z.

I will do this task that is outside of my job description with an increase to my salary or weekly pay.

I don't eat that.

I don't want another drink.

I will not get in the car with you if you are impaired.

The focus is on doing what you'd want someone who loves you to do for you. The focus is on doing the most self-loving, energy-preserving, worth-demonstrating thing for you. You are not dissuaded by the potential negative consequences or how you'll be perceived. For any change in your life to be as efficient as possible, you must take the energy you normally spend on other people's opinions or perceptions of you, and their willingness to respect your boundaries, and put it toward your change.

5. Radically Accept Yourself

Think of the change that you are currently trying to make. Do you feel an impatience or rush for it to be over so that you can feel better? If that's the case, there might be an element of attaching your state of inner peace to a changed version of yourself. And while that might be great if the version of yourself you are aiming for is your most authentic self or one that brings you closer to your desired life, it does you no good to reject your current self or reality. Read that again and let it truly sink in.

In reading the book *No Bad Parts: Healing Trauma and Restoring Wholeness with the Internal Family Systems Model* by Richard Schwartz, PhD, I learned that every part of us is working, to some extent, to either protect us or be included, seen, and validated by us. When you feel stuck and unable to do what you logically know you need to do, that is a call from your body telling you *this change you are going for is very scary.* It, in fact, threatens your body's sense of survival. So what you might perceive as lack of determination or willpower or laziness could simply be your body's way of protecting you from what it perceives to be a threat. At the same time, your body could be resisting change because, in moving forward with that change, you are rejecting certain parts of you that really want to feel included. And if you move forward without them, you move forward without being whole.

If the change you are aiming for moves you toward acceptance of your authentic self, be gentle with yourself because you are on a beautiful quest to start accepting parts of you that you thought would lead to exclusion. You are on a beautiful journey to forgive yourself and those around you for making you believe that certain parts of you made you less worthy of connection and belonging.

Radical self-acceptance does not happen at a point in the future after you've come fully into your authentic self. It happens now. It happens as you are moving toward that self. You can't shame your current self into becoming your authentic self. You love your current self into becoming your authentic self. You also can't shame past versions of yourself on your journey to your authentic self. You go back and sit with them with compassion and give them the understanding and love they needed then. Because they don't know what you know now. They are stuck back there. Your loving compassion toward them will bring them out of the shadows into parts of yourself that were learning at the time. They helped you become who you are now. Take them in and stop excluding them, because by doing so you are excluding parts of yourself. Isn't that what other people do to you at times? Don't be one of those people to yourself.

When it comes to desired goals, radical acceptance means you don't tie your "okayness" or "enoughness" to how successful you are in attaining them. When your focus is fully on the goal itself, your definition of success is fully tied to that end point. What happens if you don't reach that end point or if you reach it and it's not what you thought it was? What if you reach a different end point that is better for you, but you are fixated on that original end point? Radical acceptance of your current reality will make your journey one that truly grows you as a person because you are present for the lessons and challenges along the way. You're not just doing damage control or bypassing certain important steps just because you are so fixated on that end goal.

We are not meant to have permission to accept ourselves only once we are perfect or once our life is perfect. The only perfection we can ever reach is in accepting that our imperfections don't make us any less worthy.

Who you are now, in this moment, is 100 percent worthy of your radical acceptance. *Where* you are now, in this moment, is 100 percent worthy of your radical acceptance. This does not mean that you stay stagnant. It means that as you are working on change, you understand that the part of your life, or the part of you that you are working on changing, is exactly how it's supposed to be in this moment.

Radical acceptance will open you to being vulnerable because you aren't so caught up in proving your worth. You accept yourself and your reality in a way that allows you to be comfortable with the discomfort of taking risks and trying new things— and you can do that because you don't tie your worth to your successes or failures. Making any kind of change in life requires risks. Radical acceptance makes change inevitable because you are allowing life to flow through you instead of constantly putting up a wall of resistance to it.

I'll end with this. Repeat out loud: Accepting myself is not based on how fast I make changes for myself. Accepting myself is not dependent on what I achieve. My worthiness is here with me right now. I am the leader of my life and all the changes in it. I will take risks that might not succeed every single time. And that's okay. I will set boundaries that might make me feel uncomfortable; such discomfort doesn't mean I'm doing something wrong but that I am breaking my conditioning. I will give myself time to go through changes at my own pace and always meet myself with compassion and understanding. Starting today, I will choose for myself based on the life that I know is authentic to me. I will lead my way through the necessary changes to actualize that life. I will not wait for the pain of staying where I am to be too intense. Instead, I will choose to move toward places that nourish my growth and don't demand me to be less than myself. I will choose to move toward places that celebrate me, see me, and wholly welcome every version of me—the still-learning me, making-mistakes me, taking-risks me, and achieving-accomplishments me.

CHAPTER 8

The Beauty of Embracing Change

It's much easier to embrace a change that you actually want. I get that. But entertain this thought: When change is directly related to *your* life, perhaps it serves you to embrace what you don't choose or want. Maybe embracing it is a form of embracing the version of you that existed before this change . . . the version that was afraid this change would happen. Perhaps embracing it is a form of embracing the life you had before this change. Perhaps embracing change that we don't desire is a form of honoring our wants and needs and holding those parts of us as they go through the change.

How beautiful is it to imagine holding this life change in your arms, pulling it close like someone you care about instead of pushing it away, rejecting it, or neglecting it? Imagine picking up that change from where you pushed it aside, saying, *I don't want you.* Imagine picking it up and saying, *Even though I may not want you, I am willing to hold you as you are happening. I can grow with you, through you, and to the other side of you.*

I know it's harder to picture this when the change isn't one you want to make peace with; like the death of someone you love, losing a job you really want, or losing a relationship you thought you couldn't live without. The truth is, and I know you know this, we can't control the changes that life brings naturally. Pushing those changes away does not make them go away. It is only through radical acceptance that we can get to a place where we welcome both the sadness that comes with such changes and the will to carry on with our lives simultaneously.

Embracing change isn't about trying to trick your brain into thinking you want it. Nor is it about just acceptance or adaptation. It's about holding yourself as you go through it and trusting that you *can* get through it . . . trusting in your ability to learn new skills that will aide you along the way. You embrace change, all change, by trusting yourself. By choosing to be the leader of your life. By taking responsibility for what you need on your journey to change. By grieving when you need to. By giving yourself forgiveness and compassion. By asking for what you need and delivering that to yourself.

Though at times change might be the last thing you want, the only constant in life is that change continues to exist as long as life goes on. There's much beauty in change, and embracing it will offer you incredible gifts.

1. Embracing Change Allows You to Flow with Life

Think of the new authenticity ship you've built, the one equipped to help you sail the ocean of an authentic life. It will face storms and tides. You might struggle to navigate and end up back where you started. You might need to repair your ship at times. But you keep sailing to your destination. Imagine what would happen if a ship turned around any time a storm lay ahead or if a plane turned around any time it faced turbulence or if a car turned around any time there was slow traffic. Getting somewhere means going through challenges to get there.

Flowing with life means accepting its invitations to move forward. Sometimes moving forward looks like listening to life when it tells you to slow down, change your course of action, or take a few steps back. In the grand scheme of life and its only constant, moving forward doesn't always look like moving forward. It may sometimes mean challenging ourselves to take on new opportunities that present themselves or pursuing opportunities that could move us toward a life we really want or allowing life to take its natural course. Flowing with life sometimes means removing ourselves from a plot we realize doesn't welcome our authentic self. That might feel like regressing, but in the grand scheme of things, that's actually progressing toward an authentic life for you.

Oftentimes, what feels like regressing is really our dwelling on wanting or not wanting things to change. How many times did you contemplate making the change that's currently on your mind and, instead of actually doing something, you found yourself spending hours ruminating over how badly you want things to be different? In that ruminating, resistance is acting by making you feel stuck in your current situation instead of pushing you to do something to get out of it.

There are only twenty-four hours in a day, and every hour

you spend ruminating is an hour taken away from time you could be spending changing what your twenty-four hours look like. I don't say this with judgment, but to remind you of the power you have over your time and what you choose to invest it in.

I used to hate change. I dreaded it. I did absolutely everything to avoid it. I wanted things in my life to change without me having to alter anything. I wanted to feel better about myself without improving the way I treated myself. I wanted to feel more valued by those around me without removing myself from environments that devalued me. I would say to myself, *Can't they just see my worth?!* And the scary part was that I, myself, didn't see my worth. Because your worth, when seen and validated by you, doesn't need to be seen and validated by others. It instead moves itself toward those who see and validate it and stops begging those who don't to start doing so.

Embracing change has a lot more to do with letting go of what was than it does with holding on to what could be. The flow of life will constantly challenge us to let go and trust ourselves even when there's nothing else to hold on to in that moment. Change pushes us to let go of what once brought us comfort in some way, what felt like our survival mode, and what we perceived as necessary to our physical or emotional survival. Such necessities are like a safety blanket; it doesn't actually protect us from anything, it only grounds us in comfortable familiarity. The flow of life will pull away at that safety blanket sometimes to prompt us to live outside of our comfort zone.

Let's go back to the authenticity ship. If you drop an anchor somewhere because you want to reside there for a while, what happens if you don't release it as you're trying to sail toward a new place? You'll move a little and then be pulled back to where you were anchored. To move forward, you must release the anchors you once used to keep you attached to a place. Take a moment to reflect on this.

Another reason we resist change is that we have a hard time dealing with that space between where we are and where we want to be. It becomes harder when we don't know where we want to be, but all we know is that where we currently are doesn't feel good. And so many of us are willing to hold on to what is certain and predictable than what is vague and not guaranteed. By allowing ourselves to flow through life, we are allowing ourselves to let go of what no longer feels good and allowing space for something new to come in. How beautiful is that?

It helps to have the mindset that change, good or bad, is better than stagnancy. Making a choice, good or bad, is better than indecisiveness. There's a scene in the show *Friends* where Emily, Ross's new wife, asks him to no longer hang out with his friend Rachel, whom he used to date. She puts this as a condition for her to move forward with the marriage. For the better part of the rest of the episode, we see Ross desperately looking for the best way forward. On one hand, he could be saving his marriage, but that would mean he would never see one of his best friends ever again. His friends seem to have difficulty helping him. He becomes so desperate that he uses a Magic 8 Ball. Even the Magic 8 Ball gives him the answer "try again later." Eventually he has a conversation with Rachel without telling her about Emily's request, and Rachel tells him that he should give Emily whatever she wants. So, he tells Emily that he won't see Rachel anymore. Why am I telling you about this? Because it shows the reality of decision making and how difficult it can be. It shows how important it is to not base your decision on the opinions of those around you, but to go inward and ask yourself what you really want. And it shows the importance of moving forward with deciding instead of continuing to feel stuck, especially in situations where there are consequences to either choice. To be indecisive is worse than making a choice that comes with consequences.

So, what would you do if you were in a situation like this, where you were prompted to make a decision that has consequences both ways? Here is my advice: trust yourself. If you seek advice, make sure it's from people who are living the life you want to live and who have the same values you have. We give people a lot more power over our lives than we realize when we consult them on our decisions.

Do what, deep down, feels like it's right for you. And should you realize the choice didn't turn out the way you wanted it to, trust in your ability to move forward from it. When you lead your life with conviction and openness to imperfection and uncertainty, you become the head of the decision committee governing you.

The idea that you must guarantee that any change you make will get you the result that you want is seductive and destructive at the same time. Having a guarantee doesn't push you outside of your comfort zone. There comes a time when you just take that leap. As life flows, you have the choice to flow with it or resist it. You will sometimes feel yourself pushed or pulled in a direction different from the one you were taking. Be gentle with yourself in moments like that, and take it one small step at a time. Be flexible with it. Maybe the new direction is right. Take it into consideration before you resist it.

Part of trusting yourself is taking responsibility, account-ability, and initiative in your life. You don't wait for someone to come change your life or save you. You don't wait for someone to pick up your mess along the way. You do that yourself. And when you don't pick up the mess, you take responsibility instead of blaming others. You trust yourself as the leader of your life and act in accordance.

Write this down somewhere you can always see it: I am the leader of my life.

2. Embracing Change Allows You to Be Present

I try to be as efficient as possible with my day. While that was something I used to pride myself on, I realize now that a lot of the rush and hustle I adopted in my day-to-day life was merely an escape from the present moment. Not too long ago, I was fill-ing water in my coffee machine from the tap that dispenses filtered water. That tap dispenses much less water per second than a regular tap does. And I had this impatience in my body that wanted me to put the container in the sink and have that tap fill it up while I found something else to do. Some of you might be reading this and thinking, that's smart. It saves you some time. But the fact that I couldn't just watch water filling a container for thirty seconds revealed to me so much about not embracing the present moment and constantly feeling like any moment of stillness was a waste. I decided to challenge myself from that day to spend those thirty seconds just looking at the water filling the container without thinking about anything else. It was a meditative break for me. Do you try to escape moments in your life that are forcing you to slow down? If so, like me, you have an impatience with the simple things in life. You get caught up in the rush of things. And maybe that's thrilling because it numbs you to the reality of life. I urge you to look at those slow moments as an opportunity to be present with yourself and your reality.

One of the most common questions I get asked is, "What is your writing process?" I always felt like maybe I wasn't a real writer because I had no process. I was never able to just force myself to sit down and write any number of words because every time I did, I felt like I was forcing myself to do something I wasn't ready for. Writing has always been something that comes when it comes, not something that I can force. When I keep myself open to sitting down and being the vessel for the thoughts and emotions that come to me, I end up with the most beautiful writing. That requires an immense amount of presence. But when I try to force those thoughts and emotions to arrive before they're ready, I end up with a string of words that I eventually put a line through. Sometimes people refer to this as writer's block. I don't see it that way. I see it as the stillness that the words need before they start flowing.

I'm adopting this way of living in my everyday life. I don't try to force anything anymore. I don't try to change what I know I have no control over. I hear what people say to me, and I accept their messages for what they are instead of making excuses for them; maybe they didn't mean it that way, maybe they've had a long, hard day, or I don't believe they feel or think that way because if that were true, then it would be at odds with something else they said in the past. Living in a way where I no longer force things has allowed me to avoid being reactive. It's allowed me to be a calmer and more peaceful person who lives in reality as opposed to what I want reality to be.

I'm sure you've heard "nothing changes if nothing changes." The question is, do you want your life to change? Because once you're clear on that, the issue is the journey of change itself. If you're open enough to change to want to get to a new destination, you are more likely to be open to the little changes along the way. The impatience you might experience along the way is more akin to the impatience with the day-to-day things and our inability to be present with what we're doing. It's like we are constantly chasing after the next moment, and when the next moment arrives, we want the one after it, and so on and so forth.

One of my favorite movies is *About Time*. The main character, Tim, learns that he has the ability to go back in time. At the beginning, he uses this to manipulate the way events happened so he can get the outcome that he originally wanted. One of the most striking storylines he tries to change is his sister's, Kit, who's in an abusive relationship. The event that prompted Tim to want to change Kit's past is that she gets into an awful car accident as a result of her dealing with her abusive relationship. Tim goes back in time to the party where Kit met her abusive partner and makes sure they don't meet. Tim then comes back to the present and realizes that by altering his sister's storyline, he also altered his own; his own daughter is now his son, whom he doesn't recognize. He realizes he has to allow his sister to change her own life. He reverses the time travel and lets Kit's storyline evolve as it did before. She goes through the crash and deals with the consequences. She decides on her own to start anew. He allows her to lead her own life while he supports her through it. (An important lesson: You have to let people go through their own changes, too. As much as you want them to see what you see, you must allow them to see it on their own . . . or not.)

By the end of the movie, there is a scene that shows Tim going through a day where he wakes up in the morning, rushes to the courthouse where he works as a lawyer, goes to a coffee shop and orders coffee quickly, rushes back home, and does all the things that parents do in the evening before going to bed. And then they show a scene after that where he relives that day but this time with a focus on being present. He pays attention to the little things, his wife's face in the morning, looking at the barista making his coffee and smiling, and enjoying time with his kids. He eventually decides that he doesn't want to live a day twice to be present in it. He becomes intentional with being present every single day. He approaches each day with the presence he would usually have on the second day.

Set your intention for that now. Write this somewhere: I will be present in my life today.

3. Embracing Change Allows You to Grow into Your Authentic Self

Your perception of yourself might change if you were to let go of the image you had of yourself and contemplate that it could be different.

I always saw myself as a good girl. What that meant was I was always trying to prove that I deserved to be seen as a good girl. In letting go of past versions of myself that had no boundaries, that were people-pleasers, that were perfect, that never spoke up, and that never expressed their needs and wants, I was letting go of that title as well. And that was hard for me because I thought it meant that I was moving toward the opposite title, the one I was avoiding: a bad girl. So even though I wanted to become someone who is not a people-pleaser and saw the value in having boundaries, speaking up, being human, which meant being imperfect, and validating my permission to have my own needs and wants, I had a hard time making those changes in my life. When you look at the way you operate your life right now, what label are you attaching to the way you carry yourself? Does it mean that you are a good person? Does it mean that you are a considerate person? Does it mean that you are a good daughter, good son, hard worker, and so on? What's the title or label that you are attaching to your current way of operating in your life that you are having a hard time letting go of? Take that title and throw it away.

When I take a deep dive into what that title of good girl really meant, it was just a way to shame me into being compliant and not a burden on anyone. And by "burden," I mean that my being myself was an inconvenience to those around me. Once I was able to see that, change was something I wanted.

When you are able to tell your story in the way that you see it, as opposed to the narrative that you were fed, you're the one in charge of what comes next. This is both a scary responsibility and an exciting one. The beautiful thing about change is that it is the road to building the life you want for yourself.

I told you in the last chapter that I always had a hard time letting go of moments of connection I had with people and that I had a hard time with them changing their minds about how they felt about me. And how that bred an insufferable desperation in me to hold on to the past because of how connected I felt in those moments. Not only did that mean that I lived in the past, escaping my present constantly, but also that I held on to past versions of myself. The reason most of those relationships fell apart was that I was showing more and more of my true self. I was beginning to have standards and expectations. I was beginning to express my wants and needs. I was becoming less of a people-pleaser and more of a person who doesn't survive by pleasing others. If that's the only way those relationships existed, wanting to go back to those relationships entails an element of wanting to go back to the version(s) of me that upheld those relationships.

Embracing change means I must consciously choose myself over my relationships with others when those two are at odds. This doesn't just apply to relationships. It applies to jobs, life stages, where you live—you name it. Anything that requires you to sacrifice who you are is not worth it. At the end of the day, you don't want to live a life that only works if you pretend to be someone you're not.

Embracing change through presence with yourself means leaving versions of you in the past and leaving future versions of you in the future. Leaving them doesn't mean you reject them. They are always with you. Leaving them means not allowing them to lead you in the present. They can sit in the passenger seat or back seat of your car. But only you are the driver. Don't judge yourself based on how far you are from your ideal self. Your ideal self is here right now. You can't grow into someone you're chasing. You grow into someone you're becoming.

Most of the tears I cried in my life were over things that changed. They were over things I thought I wanted to stay the same. But when I look back at those times and imagine going back to what I had before, I feel gratitude in my heart that change happened. I remember having a conversation with my therapist when I was expressing how upsetting it was to me that all the moments in my life where I made decisions for myself happened at the point where the pain of staying the same was so much worse than the pain of changing. And I think that is an under-discussed topic. We think that something has to be really bad for us to have permission to say, "I don't want this." We let things get to a point where it's not about what we want but about what we can no longer survive. While that's effective motivation, it sets a very dangerous standard. Embracing change gives us permission to change our lives out of choice, not out of having no other option.

Embracing change means living your life in the way that feels best for you. For example, embracing change could look like saying no to going out because you recognize that the place is just not where you want to be, or saying no to an opportunity because you are happy with where you currently are, and owning that. Embracing change doesn't mean you change yourself to fit into the world around you. It means allowing your authentic self to *be* and being okay with the world around you reacting and changing as a result. Owning your choices is essential. Embracing change means embracing the person you authentically are and protecting your peace at any cost, setting boundaries, speaking your mind, and letting some relationships go.

There's a price to pay for every change you need to make but don't. When you hold back on making a needed change, it is not simply that you are standing still. You are choosing to continue living in a way that moves you farther away from the life you know you want to live. This doesn't mean that something is wrong with you. It just means that you are confining yourself to the limits of what you thought was your survival mode. It takes a series of little steps, little pushes against that border, the limits of your survival mode, to get over that edge. And once you're on the other side, even though you may feel like an exile and don't belong or fit in, you'll know that you survived. You survived what you never thought you could survive. You survived what you have been so terrified of for so long. Once you are living proof that your survival mode isn't representative of the life you can live and that, in fact, it is the most caging version of the life you can live, you yourself will want to be in exile from that life. Once you taste the beauty of making it on your own and actually surviving, you will want that solitude.

Write this down somewhere: I want to get to the other side of my survival mode.

4. Embracing Change Allows You to Move from Having Things Happen *to* You to Making Things Happen *for* You

I was walking with one of my close friends at the park about three years ago. We were walking slowly and enjoying the brisk air and the sound of leaves. There was a slight breeze, and it was just heavenly. I was talking about how grateful I was to have become the person I wanted to be. I then started to talk about the number of people who walked out of my life or who started treating me in a way that very clearly showed that they judged me. And all of a sudden, the exclusion and loneliness that I felt as a result of that kind of treatment bubbled up to the surface, and I started feeling tension all over my body. I abruptly stomped my feet very loudly as I said, "But if my life wasn't as bad as it was before, I wouldn't have had to change it so much!" As I said this, part of me felt like a victim for being raised with a heavy religious background, being so sheltered and inexperienced in life and love, and for growing up in a culture that is very much shame-driven, where talking about feelings is taboo. My thought process was, if that wasn't my reality, I wouldn't have had to break out of it. And as a result, I wouldn't have had to deal with the exclusion that came with me breaking out of it.

I really was expecting my friend to say, "Yes, I understand how hard that must have been." Instead, he said, "But now you know who you are. You are either going to continue living that life or choose differently for yourself. And choosing differently for yourself required you to question that reality. And once you questioned it, you realized you wanted differently for yourself. And you actually did something about it. Do you know how hard that is? So many people get stuck in the realization part and spend their lives suffering. I'm not telling you to be grateful for the pain, but I'm telling you to be grateful to yourself for choosing differently. And for choosing based on who you are, not who you were taught you needed to be."

Those are the words I needed to tell myself. The truth is that no matter how strong you become and how much conviction you have in the life that you created for yourself, you will still go through moments when you will stomp your feet and say, "But if that didn't happen to me, I wouldn't be dealing with this right now." That happens because you are human. Something hurting isn't always an indication that it is wrong for you. Sometimes the hurting is actually an indication that you are doing something right for yourself. It hurts to have to do it alone. It hurts to choose for yourself when you've never done so and to trust yourself when you've always doubted yourself. It's uncomfortable. You will go through many moments where you will wish that your reality didn't push you to a point where you had to make change. In moments like that, I want you to remember: Don't give the credit for your change to how bad your reality was. Give the credit for your change to yourself, to the person who woke up one day and decided, "This reality doesn't honor my authentic self. This reality doesn't make me feel wholly welcome and worthy. This reality doesn't see me for who I am and doesn't hear my voice, let alone listen to it." Give the credit for your change to the person you are becoming. To the person who refused to continue living in victimhood hoping that others will feel bad for you and come save you. Give the credit to the person who decided to stop having things happen to them and started making things happen for yourself.

Give the credit for who you are now to yourself. Even as you are working to become the best version of yourself, which is your most authentic self, give yourself credit for choosing to pave your own path. Even if you feel like the person you are now isn't nearly as strong, confident, or well put together as you would like to be, who you are right now deserves the same kind of celebration and accolades as who you are becoming. Because both of those people are one; you. Just like you no longer want to surround yourself with people who don't accept you as you are, you don't want to be with yourself if you don't accept yourself as you are. Just like you no longer want to surround yourself with people who need you to have a certain status, job, financial situation, or stage in life for them to welcome, respect, or love you, you also wouldn't want to welcome, respect, and love yourself without those external life milestones. You need to see the person inside of you who is trying their absolute best. You need to hear the voice of the person inside of you who is screaming for understanding. That is the person who deserves to take all the credit for all the changes you chose.

Write this down somewhere: I give myself credit for all the changes I've made in my life.

5. Embracing Change Transforms Your Life

To embrace change is to live a life where you put belonging over fitting in. You no longer focus your efforts on the world around you to make it welcome you. That goes against what authentic change looks like. Even if the change you're aiming for has to do with a job, school program, or reaching any milestone in life, if your aim is changing how others perceive you, your change is outwardly focused. You need to make the change because it's something you want, not because it's something that will make you feel welcomed, respected, or loved by others.

To embrace change is to live in radical acceptance of yourself and your life, even as you're changing. Radical acceptance doesn't mean weakness or submission. It means not resisting, rejecting, or being in denial of your reality. Embracing change allows you to approach life without reacting or making everything mean something about you. You see life as it is and accept it. You see yourself as you are and accept yourself. You don't want to be working toward becoming someone you would currently reject. Aim to not make your current self someone who, in five years, you have to apologize to for being so hard on them.

To embrace change is to no longer settle for conditional love and not accept anything less than whole love. It is to look at the love that others have to offer and see it for what it is instead of confining yourself to how willing they are to love you the way you need to be loved. It is no longer talking yourself out of the validity of your needs and wants based on what they're willing to offer you. It is to no longer try to change yourself so that their love toward you changes. Embracing change means accepting the choices that others make for themselves, especially when those choices involve you and their treatment of you. To embrace change is to allow your authentic self to shine through and break the conditioning that told you that you need to be and do certain things to be worthy. It is allowing yourself to break out of the survival mode that makes you act out of fear of being abandoned or losing people, and moving outside that survival mode into full, whole, authentic-life mode.

To embrace change is to stop conforming to who you thought you needed to be in order to become who you authentically are. It is to go in life toward what feeds your soul, toward what makes you happy. From a young age, we are surrounded with messaging that tells us what we need to grow up to be, what kind of education we need to have, what kind of job we need to have, at what age we need to be married and have children, own a house, and so on. To embrace change is to question the rules that family, society, culture, and religion placed on you and to allow yourself to break those rules when they are at odds with your authentic truth. You are not meant to live your life in a way where you fit into a mold. You are meant to live your life in a way where the world around you hugs your shape without constricting you or chiseling you down and embraces you as you are, not as you should be.

To accept change is not always to be okay with it or celebrate it. Change isn't always beautiful. It isn't always for the better. Sometimes change takes away people we love, including versions of ourselves. Sometimes change takes our health, our family, our dreams, and more. To acknowledge it doesn't mean to be okay with it. To accept change is sometimes to radically accept reality, to admit to ourselves that we would really love for our reality to be different. To get back what we lost. To turn back time and allow us more time with what we lost, with those we lost. To embrace change is sometimes to embrace what we lost, and those we lost, through the change and after it. To continue to express love and gratitude to what was once our reality and to make space for it in our current one. To embrace change isn't always easy or comfortable. That's why we must honor our process, allow our grief to flow through us, and be compassionate with ourselves through life's only constant.

To embrace change is to lead your life instead of being a follower. It is to be the writer of your story, the narrator and the main character in it. To embrace change is to become a person of choice, someone who doesn't wait for things to get so bad before giving yourself permission to make a choice for yourself. It is to be yourself even when that means you stand out from the crowd. Even when that means that you become an inconvenience or a burden on others, in their views. To embrace change is to allow those who only accept you when you are a follower to continue on the paths they lead while you break off and pave a path of your own. To embrace change is to understand that it is not having followers that makes you a leader; it is leading your life with decisions, responsibility, initiative, and autonomy. You can be a leader on your own and have people walk with you as they lead their own paths.

As we come to the end of this book, I have a confession to make. I lied to you about one thing. Change is not the only constant in life. *You* are the only constant in *your* life. Yes, you. You are the only one who's been there with you and for you since the moment you were born. You're the only one who's had to endure what you've gone through from the moment you took your first breath on this earth. You are the only person in your life who wakes up with you every morning and goes to bed with you every night. You are the one who breathed your way through the tough moments and laughed your soul out through the beautiful ones. Navigate your way through *life's* only constant by embracing that you are *your* only constant. One day, you will look back at the life you lived and say, "I lived a life that was authentic to me. And I am proud of that. Through the good, the bad, and everything in between, I stayed true to myself."

How beautiful is that?

What are you waiting for? Start now.

ACKNOWLEDGMENTS

Writing this book wouldn't have been possible without all the changes and people in my life.

I want to thank every person who walked out of my life after promising they wouldn't. You taught me that people change and things don't always stay the same. And that is a blessing. As long as I don't walk away from myself, I'm okay.

I want to thank every person who lied to me. You taught me that no amount of effort I expend will change someone else. All I can change is myself. I can embrace my honesty.

I want to thank every person who turned their back on me. You taught me that expecting others to treat me with the same loyalty I treat them with is unrealistic. I will always have my own back.

I also want to thank every person who stayed. You showed me how beautiful unconditional love is as we change and evolve into our best selves.

I want to thank every person who always shared the truth

with me. You helped me grow, be creative, and feel safe taking risks.

I want to thank every person who stood up for me and supported me when I needed them. You empowered me and provided a safe environment for me to heal.

I also want to thank every past version of me who resisted change and struggled to accept it. I am here because you made it through.

I want to thank my family, friends, and loved ones for loving me in your own way through all my changes.

I want to thank my editor, Donna, for walking with me and guiding me as I share my journey with the world.

And my team at Penguin Random House for working tirelessly to help me spread my work around the world.

And Katie for your consistent loyalty and advocacy.

And Marc and Tess for always believing in me and what sets me apart from the rest.

ABOUT THE AUTHOR

Najwa Zebian, Ed.D., is a Lebanese Canadian activist, author, speaker, and educator with a doctorate in educational leadership. Dr. Zebian began to write in an effort to connect with and heal her first students, a group of young refugees. The author of four books that guide readers to navigate hard emotions, most recently *Welcome Home*, Dr. Zebian delivered the TEDx talk "Finding Home Through Poetry." She recently launched her podcast, *In the Clear*, with cohost Stephan Maighan to guide listeners in gaining clarity through a holistic look through logic and emotion. Her work has been featured in *The New York Times*, *Glamour*, *Elle Canada*, *HuffPost*, and more.

Also by Najwa Zebian

Welcome Home
A Guide to Building a Home For Your Soul

In *Welcome Home*, Zebian shares her story for the first time, powerfully weaving memoir, poetry and deeply resonant teachings into her storytelling, from leaving Lebanon at sixteen, to coming of age as a young Muslim woman in Canada, to building a new identity for herself as she learned to speak her truth. After the profound alienations she experienced, she learned to build a stable foundation inside herself, an identity independent of cultural expectations and the influence of others. With practical tools and prompts for self-understanding, she shows you how to build each room in your house, which form a firm basis for your self-worth, sense of belonging and happiness.

Trade Paperback 978 1 473 69999 1
ebook 978 1 529 33651 1
audiobook 978 1 399 72063 2

books to help you live a good life

Join the conversation and tell
us how you live a #goodlife

🐦 @yellowkitebooks
📘 YellowKiteBooks
📌 Yellow Kite Books
📷 YellowKiteBooks